M000106481

ANIMAL ARMS

Ultimate Size and Shape Training for Building Monstrous Arm Muscles

Copyright © 1996 by Robert Kennedy

All rights reserved, including the right to
reproduce this book or portions thereof
in any form whatsoever.

Published by MuscleMag International
6465 Airport Road
Mississauga, Ontario
Canada L4V 1E4

Designed by Jackie Kydyk

Canadian Catalguing in Publication Data

Kennedy, Robert, 1938-
    Animal arms: ultimate size and shape training
for building monstrous arm muscles

Includes bibliographical references and index.

    1. Bodybuilding--Training. I.Hines, Dwayne,
1961- II. Title.

GV546.5.K448 1996   646.7'5   C96-900752-3

ISBN 1-55210-004-9

10 9 8 7 6 5 4 3 2 1

Distributed in Canada by
MuscleMag International
6465 Airport Road
Mississauga, Ontario
Canada L4V 1E4

Distributed in the United States by
MuscleMag International
(Swan Screening)
1789 South Park Avenue
Buffalo, NY
USA 14220

Printed in Canada

*This book is dedicated to Janet, and to
Tim Mills and Jeff Taylor, with whom I spent
many hours in arm training.*

This book is not intended as medical advice, nor is it offered for use in the diagnosis of any health condition or as a substitute for medical treatment and/or counsel. Its purpose is to explore advanced topics on sports nutrition and exercise. All data are for information only. Use of any of the programs within this book is at the sole risk and choice of the reader.

Contents

Jay Cutler

About the Authors

Robert Kennedy is one of the most knowledgeable and respected authorities in bodybuilding. He has written dozens of books on bodybuilding including the best-sellers *Hardcore Bodybuilding*, *Beef It!*, *Pumping Up* (co-authored by Ben Weider), and *Reps!*. He is also the publisher of *MuscleMag International*, a monthly magazine for male and female bodybuilders which he started in 1974.

Robert Kennedy has trained for many years and has competed successfully in both weightlifting and bodybuilding contests. He was born in England in 1938 and emigrated to Canada at the age of 30. He was trained as an artist specializing in oil painting and stone carving and, to this day, keeps up with both.

Dwayne Hines II was active as an athlete from his youth and gravitated toward bodybuilding. He has participated in bodybuilding as a competitor, personal trainer and physique competition judge. His articles on bodybuilding have appeared in national magazines for the past 13 years and his general training articles have been published in a variety of magazines outside of the sport. Dwayne has served in the military and is also a martial artist. He is the president of Iron Mountain Enterprises, a marketing firm in Meridian, Idaho.

Lee Labrada

Chapter One

Building Massive Arm Muscles

When it comes to overall impression, the arm muscles are the most popular muscles on the body. When you hear the term "show me your muscles," you do not necessarily think of your lower back muscles, your shoulder muscles or any other somewhat obscure muscle group – you think of your arm muscles. One top physique star, **Aaron Baker**, noted that he often hears "Hey Aaron! Make a muscle!" Aaron also points out "if I had a dollar for every time I heard that from friends, relatives and kids on the street, I'd own Gold's Gym. What does make a muscle mean? To a non-bodybuilder it means flexing your biceps. If there were a popularity contest among the body's muscle groups, biceps would win hands (and arms) down!"[1]

Arnold Schwarzenegger recognizes the same phenomenon. In *Arnold: The Education of a Bodybuilder* he points out "to some people the biceps are the symbol of strength. Everybody can relate to arms. Arms are one of the most impressive parts of the body, the part everybody wants to see. When somebody says 'Show me your muscles,' you don't show your calves. You automatically lift your arm and flex your biceps. A lot of attention should be put into the arms so they look good."[2]

The arms hold a certain mystique of power – as Arnold mentioned, they are a symbol of strength. The arms convey a sense of power and muscularity. The great poet, Henry Wadsworth Longfellow, captured the human fascination with the power of the arm in the poem "The Village Blacksmith."

> **Under the spreading chestnut tree**
> **The village smithy stands;**
> **The smith a mighty man is he**
> **With large and sinewy hands.**
> **And the muscles of his brawny arms**
> **Are strong as iron bands.**

Longfellow is not the only writer to use the arm to convey a sense of power. The Bible refers to the strength of God by using statements such as "the mighty arm of the Lord." As Arnold mentioned, the arm is truly a symbol of strength and power. Mass is the primary sign of a powerful arm. People notice the arms. For instance, **Don Long**, the 1995 NPC National Champion was reported to have "hit paydirt last year with a pair of 21-inch guns that resembled inflated brown boulders. Whenever Long raised his mighty arms in that stylish front double biceps shot, the crowd cheered him on. Peaked pillars of power best describe the flexed arms."[3] When fully developed, the arms are awesome and turn heads.

Shape is an important factor in the appearance of the arm. It is not enough to have

Aaron Baker

Lee Labrada, Vince Taylor and Shawn Ray

a big, massive, powerful arm. The arm should also have some symmetry for full effect. It can have that shape if you train it correctly. Proper training (along with diet, rest and recuperation) is how you add size and shape to your arm. The training also includes the right effort – high-intensity all-out effort. You need to have all the information on training your arms, and then put that information together into a powerful drive to add to the size and shape of your arms. This book, *Animal Arms*, will provide you with all the information about arm size and shape that you need to build brawny arms.

Arnold Schwarzenegger aptly describes the muscles and functions of the upper arm in his autobiography:

The upper arm is made up of two muscle groups – the biceps and the triceps. As the prefix "bi" implies, the biceps has two parts. The short head arises from a tendon attached to the coronoid process of the scapula and inserts into the upper portion of the radius bone of the forearm. It aids in the flexion of the upper arm, shoulder, and forearm. The long head of the biceps originates from the supra glenoid tuberosity of the upper arm bone and inserts in a common tendon sheath with the short head into the forearm. Its major function is the flexion

of the forearm. The triceps is composed of three muscles with a common tendonous attachment – hence the name triceps. The long head arises from a tendon on the scapula; the lateral from the posterior surface of the upper arm (humerus) bone; and the medial head has its origin in an area just below that of the lateral head. All three insert into a single tendon attached to the forearm. The action of the triceps is to extend the forearm, with the long head also aiding in bringing the arm closer to the body from a lateral position.[4]

There is also another muscle that plays an important part in arm size – the brachialis muscle. The brachialis is a broad and relatively flat band of muscle tissue which lies between the biceps and the upper arm bone(humerus).[5] In addition to the upper arm, a well-developed lower arm (forearm) is also essential for full arm strength, power and appearance.

Animal Arms will focus on all three of the muscle groups that make up the arms. An arm that has only one group fully developed is out of balance. To be totally awesome, an arm needs to be completely developed. A complete focus of prioritized training will be directed at the arms (biceps, triceps, and forearm) to take them far beyond their current level of develop-

Lee Haney

Arnold Schwarzenegger

adequate passion. You have to become an animal in the gym to get the awesome arms you want. So go ahead and be a nice person outside of the gym, but in the gym, become an *animal!*

Passion and Intensity

This book will provide you with the necessary information to take your arm development to a higher level. But you must have one thing if you want the information to work for you – **passion**. You must have a deep and strong passion for developing your physique, particularly your arms. Without training passion you might as well quit. People get passionate about a myriad of different things. You have to get passionate about your body specifically, your arms. Passion gets you to the gym on a stormy

ment. Various exercises, several specific arm routines, inside training tips, ideas from champions who have great arms, and effective arm expansion techniques will be presented in a logical, concise format so that you can use this information to add more muscle size and shape to your arms. The more knowledge you have to work with, the better "armed" you are. The *"animal"* aspect refers to the training intensity that is required to reach beyond your current level of arm development and build big biceps, tremendous triceps and ferocious forearms.

Big, beautiful arms are not free; they don't grow on trees. You cannot get a pair of massively muscular arms just because you are a nice person. In fact, being nice (in the gym) won't cut it. The only way the arms will give way to your desire for more size and shape is through force. The only language the body understands when it comes to growth is force. You have to literally force your body to become what you want it to be. You have to get nasty with yourself and push past the pain barrier to reach that training zone where the growth is stimulated. This can only occur if you have

ANIMAL ARMS ANIMAL ARMS ANIMAL ARMS ANIMAL ARMS

night when the weather is questionable. Passion gets you through a workout when you would like to go watch football. Passion provides a reason for training. And passion shows itself in the gym through intensity. It takes a high level of intensity and consistency to build big and shapely arms, and if you don't have passion for building your physique you won't have a chance of generating the intensity and consistency that will take you to a level of super development.

Craig Titus

Intensity is the path upon which your arms travel to new levels of size and shape. Without intensity in your training you are really just wasting your time. A workout without intensity is a futile exercise of merely going through the motions. Mediocre, half-hearted training will not provide the stimulus to take your arms to awesome new size. Mr. Olympia, **Dorian Yates**, says "getting bigger means toughing it out in the gym."[6] And if anyone would know, it would be Dorian. He has systematically improved every year by using extremely intense, tough workouts. You have to do the same if you expect to have awesome arms. **You cannot get to an extreme level of arm development without extreme workouts!** The equation is quite simple. Light arm workouts produce light arms. Average arm workouts produce average arms. And intense arm workouts produce *animal arms.*

Your arms won't change unless you give them a very good reason to. That reason comes through super-hot intensity in the gym. You have to literally "bomb" your biceps, triceps, and forearms to make change happen. Intensity is the vehicle that makes it happen. Intensity is the key to positive change in any sporting endeavor – bodybuilding is no exception. You have to make the arms "burn" to effect a difference in them. Intensity needs to be part of each and every workout in order to build *animal arms.* Champion bodybuilder **Milos Sarcev** (a.k.a Mishko) is a firm believer in passionate intensity. An article noted that "for Mishko, the main thing is intensity. The secret for building massive muscles is high intensity. It doesn't matter how strict your form is or how many sets you do – if intensity is low you are not going to grow."[7] **Craig Titus** is another behemoth who believes in a high-voltage workout. He applies intensity to each set and "goes ballistic."[8] If you examine how the champion bodybuilders train, you will find that they are more intense than the average person in the gym. You need to follow their lead if you expect to build arms that stand out.

If you want to build a "nasty body," you have to train intensely. That especially applies to the arms. When it comes to building *animal arms*, high-intensity training on a consistent basis separates the men from the boys. For instance, it is not unusual to have several guys show up for the first workout with Mr. Clean, **Dr. Ollie McClay**, (21+ inch arms at an age over 50) and have that number reduced by more than two-thirds for the next workout because many can't handle the pain of his "no mercy workouts." You can't be a "boy" or a gym pansy and expect to have huge arms. You have to put in some heavy duty, high-intensity workouts to get any real arm size.

M & M

How do you generate passion? How do you build up sufficient intensity? You do so through the use of motivation and momentum – M & M – the twin elements of making something happen. Passion should be a natural outflow of your personal desires. To be successful in building your body, you have to be passionate about it. This passion will generate a certain momentum that feeds on itself.

If you really want to build awesome arms, then you should have a motivation for doing whatever is necessary to reach your goals. Continual motivation will generate momentum. The combination of motivation and the resulting momentum is a powerful, intangible force that will heat your passion to a very high level and give you the fire to remain sustained through those tough workouts. You will find that your hesitancy will disappear as your workouts become more productive. Your tough workouts will become something that you look forward to and even are addicted to. The more success you have in building your arm muscles and adding shape, the more excited you will become about training your arms. This will in turn cause a "snowball" effect which will take your training passion even higher. And a high level of training passion will ignite an intensity that will enable you to burn through your workouts with success. Training motivation and training momentum have an effect that is awesome – and they feed on each other once you get them started. If you can get into the "M & M groove," using motivation to spur momentum, your growth gains will take off like a rocket. Passionate, intense, heavy-duty workouts will become a habit instead of a hit-and-miss event. The more intense your workouts are, the more growth you will generate in your arms.

Vince Taylor

The concept of bringing passion to your training is far more important than any little "secret" weight training tip! A person with passion for building great arms will soon surpass someone who has no real passion but knows a couple of supposed weird little training secrets. The person with passion will stay at the task until he succeeds. If he is not getting immediate result, he will continue to search and train until he does. If he doesn't have the knowledge, he will keep looking and experimenting until he finds it. And he will blast his arms until they have no other option but to grow. The most certain key for success in building the body (and more directly, the arms) is a combination of passion and knowledge. This book will provide the knowledge, *but you have to supply the passion.* Knowledge is very important, but only if you use it passionately. Think about your goal and dream of having awesome arms – *animal arms* and push as hard as you can toward that goal. If you want it you can get it if you do the right things. Read this book to learn what to do, then do it with everything you've got. Take the knowledge and bomb away in the gym.

Applied Knowledge

Many people will state that "knowledge is power." Wiser people have pointed out that statement is not really true. It is "applied knowledge" that is power. That is especially true for bodybuilding. Unless you apply the knowledge that you have, and apply it with passion, you will not see any significant results. It is important that you apply the training techniques, and inside information, that you learn in *Animal Arms*. Don't apply the training techniques in a half-hearted manner. Get into the workout with a ferocious intensity. Apply what you learn with all the fire you have inside. But do it wisely. Make your intensity a controlled intensity. For instance, if you workout on your arms every day you will quickly cease to make gains because you are overtraining. If you control your intensity and train your arms as hard as possible once every few days, your arms will really grow. Use your intensity in a wise manner, and intelligently apply all the knowledge you can get.

Always be willing to incorporate new information when it comes to training the body. The top bodybuilders continually research what is happening in the sport of bodybuilding to stay abreast of current developments and ahead of everyone else. Even Mr. Olympia, **Dorian Yates,** uses new research and innovation to make new gains.[9] Get as much knowledge as you can, and apply it in the gym to find out what will assist you in building *animal arms*.

Your Mind

Training your arms is not a "no-brainer." You have to do some thinking. **Lee Haney** points out that "bodybuilding today is a science, and you'd better be prepared to research your subject and get your act together if you want to progress."[10] Contrary to the false impression that some athletes have, building the body is also a mental process. Nothing replaces good-old common sense. You will also develop a personal physique intuition, a type of sixth sense that will let you know how your body is responding, or not responding, to certain types of

Charles Clairmonte, Flex Wheeler and Michael Francois.

training and dietary practices. Try all of the training techniques listed in *Animal Arms.* Use those that work; toss out those that don't. Think through the reasons why some exercises are working and others are not. Plan your training program. Use *Animal Arms* as a training guide to lead you to the right path to the massive, muscular arms you want. Be daring enough to adapt the training techniques to your own routine. No two bodies are exactly the same. Yours may respond differently to some exercise or repetition range than does your training partner's. Exercise and diet adaptation are crucial for custom-tailoring the general workout into a specific workout that works for you. Use *Animal Arms* as a training manual that provides general guidelines for your own personal adaptation. View the book as a "cookbook" for serving up arm size and shape (use the general recipes but feel free to add a little extra "spice" where you feel it is necessary). However, try each of the given techniques for a sufficient time before making a freelance move. Always, use your mind! It is your most important muscle when it comes to training the body. It is the mind, not the body, that determines when you will quit, or if you will persist.

Total Training

The arms should be viewed as a full unit made up of three major muscle groups, not one or two. You do not want to make the mistake of focusing too much on one of the arm muscle groups to the detriment of the others. Some people focus all of their attention on the biceps. Since the biceps is the "show" muscle of the body, it is natural to aim a lot of training effort at this muscle group. However, if taken to the extreme, the results are ridiculous. Imagine an arm were the biceps are massive and the triceps and forearm are relatively small in comparison. The arm would look "freakish" in a bad way. Or the reverse could be true – huge triceps and no biceps or forearm size. Either is unattractive. There must be a balance, a symmetry to the arms. And this does not only apply to the biceps and triceps, but also to the forearms. Popeye the Sailorman has huge forearms and a small upper arm, and he looks silly. Unbalanced development is strange. To get it right, the three muscle groups of the arm,

the biceps, triceps, and forearm, all need to compliment each other.

Make certain to give equal attention to each of the three major muscle groups of the arm. Make your arm training "total" training. The one exception is the person who has forearms that develop rapidly from any arm training. These fortunate individuals have genetics that cause their forearms to develop when they are performing other exercises where gripping the bar is used, and this provides enough stimulation for their forearms to grow to significant muscular proportions. Most people are not so fortunate and they need to directly work on their forearms. Plan on spending time working your forearm muscles. Chapter four will focus on the concepts, tips, and training for the forearms.

Lee Haney

Overtraining

One of the very real problems for training the arms is that of overtraining. Overtraining means too much training – going over the necessary amount of stimulus for muscle growth. Unfortunately, it is fairly easy to overtrain the arms since they are a popular muscle group and a lot of people focus on

Albert Beckles

them. Overtraining is most common with the biceps (but some people also make the mistake with their triceps training). People pump out set after set on this muscle, and usually end up hindering their progress with misplaced zeal. The general rule is that the smaller muscle groups of the body need fewer exercises and sets, and the larger muscle groups can handle more exercises and sets. There are some exceptions such as the calves, but in general this rule is a good one. Yet many people violate the rule by performing vast amounts of exercises and sets and wonder why their biceps are not growing. The logical conclusion is that they have taken their muscles beyond the growth zone and into an overtrained condition. This happens quite frequently, especially with the novice. The novice tries to solve a training problem by throwing more sets at a muscle

group that has ceased to respond and then he adds even more sets. He is throwing his arms into such a shocked, overtrained condition that the progress is nil. This causes all kinds of problems. Overtraining is the enemy of progress, especially with the smaller body parts such as the arms. Many of the champion bodybuilders, the guys with the great big guns, have figured this out and spend a lot less time on the arms. **Larry Scott** uses a quick but intense workout. **Lee Labrada**, a top champion and professional bodybuilder for the past nine years, amazingly uses only six to nine sets total for all of his biceps exercises.[11] Not very much when you consider that some people use five times that amount. **Lee Haney** said that he had to be aware of sliding into the overtraining mode when he revamped his arm workout. He says overtraining the arms (especially the biceps) is a particularly easy thing to do.[12] When you train the arms it is important to remember that they are a smaller muscle group and work them accordingly. Trainers caution to error on the side of too few sets rather than too many for the smaller muscle groups. The arm training routines presented in *Animal Arms* will use the approach of working on a smaller muscle group so that you can get maximum growth. Of course, a higher set scheme, is perfectly fine as an occasional "shock" cycle so long as this type of training is not typical.

The Growth Zone

The key to arm growth is to get a highly intense workout in just a few sets. This means that you have to push yourself into the growth zone – the dimension of training where muscle pain is constant – to get results. To achieve this, you have to use a weight that gets so heavy in the last 2 to 4 repetitions that the pain is almost unbearable. The pain that hurts so bad (make certain the pain is in the muscles and not the joints, bone, or ligaments) is what will produce the muscle size. The repetitions performed with weights that are too light to cause this pain are not very productive. If you always train at a level less than intense, you should not expect massive arms. **Arnold Schwarzenegger** pointed out in the movie *Pumping Iron* that the ability to handle the pain at this intense level separates those who succeed in bodybuilding and those who are just average. If you can't get into the growth zone for a couple of repetitions, you won't make any real progress. The growth zone is where you will change the size and shape of your arms. Go for the growth zone with every set of every workout. You can rest after the workout (and you need to spend a lot of time resting) but not during the workout.

You can also hit the growth zone with a shock workout – an unusual training tool where you depart from your regular training approach. This may include five times as many sets as normal, or a doubling of the amount of repetitions. You do not want to push into this growth zone too often because you can get into an overtrained state quickly.

The Formula

In training the arms you do not want to overtrain or undertrain. The growth zone is between too small an amount of stimulation (too few sets, repetitions, and exercises with too much rest) and too much of an overload (too many sets, repetitions, and exercises with not enough rest). **The formula for building massive muscle size and shape is to train very intensely (with the last few repetitions of each set in the pain zone) for a few sets of a few exercises, with an occasional variation of more sets and exercises for a short period of time.**

It may take you a bit of trial-and-error to find your exact growth zone, but use the parameters listed above to find out where you fit. And don't cheat yourself! You know when you are going all out, and you know when you are letting yourself off easy. The only thing you

Michael Francois and Flex Wheeler

Ronnie Coleman

apply the growth formula to. This book will present many of the very best biceps, triceps and forearm training exercises as well as the key training and essential growth principles for each muscle group that will make your arms more muscular. A complete chapter will be devoted to each of these individual muscle groups so that you have plenty of ammunition available when you go to the gym or garage to work on your arms. The workouts and specific routines that the champion bodybuilders used to make their arms awesome will also be included, along with some super tips for maximum arm size and strength gains.

If you use these training principles and techniques you can build *animal arms*. That is, you can succeed at making your arm muscles more massive and contoured if you use applied knowledge and have hot passion for reaching your goals.

Read through the entire book before beginning to use the principles for building *animal arms*. It is best to get a good grasp of the overall arm training process before starting to get your program planned out. Take notes as you read each section. Write down ideas that you think will be effective for training your arms. Also take

do when you come up short of a full workout is cheat your arms out of the necessary stimulation that they need to grow. Remember, every time you cheat in a workout by not going into the growth zone you only make it longer until you get to where you want to go.

There is a real variety, dozens and dozens, of different arm exercises available to

notes in your training diary as to what works best for you as you try the different arm training strategies. Keep what works, get rid of what doesn't. Build your own knowledge base about your own arms. Your arms may respond slightly differently than the next bodybuilders, so find out what works and what doesn't. Use this book, as a guide to find the best possible routine for you. And don't stop at one. Although some people like **Larry Scott** use the same arm routine for years, others benefit from having more than one "hot" routine. Whatever you do, do it all-out.

The Animal Arms motto for each workout. Go hard or go home!

It all comes down to the simple fact of how badly you want awesome *animal arms*. If you want something badly enough you won't let anything stand in your way. You must and will find the necessary knowledge, and then you will apply that knowledge in a super hot intense manner to achieve your goal. **Lou Ferrigno**, the Incredible Hulk and massive bodybuilder, believes he actually "willed" himself to become a champion. The same approach is necessary if you wish to have incredible arms. You have to want it so badly that you take all the necessary steps to make it happen. Read through the following chapters and find the steps to *animal arms.*

Lou Ferrigno

Dorian Yates

1. Aaron Baker, "Deliberate Contractions," *Flex*, August 1990, p.63
2. Arnold Schwarzenegger and Douglas Kent Hall, "Arnold: The Education of a Bodybuilder." New York: Wallaby Pocket Books, 1977, p. 215
3. Reg Bradford, "Peaked Pillars of Power," *Muscular Development*, March 1996, p. 73
4. Schwarzenegger p.215
5. Bertil Fox, "Mountains from Molehills," *Flex*, August 1990, p. 18
6. Peter McGough, "Out of the Shadow," *Flex*, August 1992, p.80
7. Greg Zulak, "The way to Balanced Arms," *MuscleMag International*, June 1993, p. 20
8. Greg Zulak, "Titan Workouts for Terrific Triceps," *MuscleMag International*, April 1995, p. 172
9. Peter McGough, p. 76
10. Lee Haney with Peter McGough, "Making up the Lee Way," *MuscleMag International*, May 1988, p. 58
11. Greg Zulak, "Lee Labrada Biceps," *MuscleMag International*, May-June 1991, pp. 54-60
12. Lee Haney with Peter McGough, p. 59

Francois Muse

The arm muscles are the show muscles of the physique. When someone asks to "see your muscles," they are most likely referring to your arms, and more specifically, your biceps. The arms are one of the most visible muscle groups (perhaps more visible than any other except the neck). That in and of itself should be motivating enough to make your arm muscles sharp. One of the keys to having awesome looking arms is to have great biceps.

Lee Labrada

A well-developed biceps takes on the appearance of a mountain. From the low at each end of the muscle, a trained biceps sweeps high into the air, peaking at a marked point. Even in a non-flexed or contracted state, a big biceps is

Chapter Two

The Biceps: Mountains of Muscle

impressive. The impression a massive biceps gives is that of massive strength.

Except for very few genetically gifted individuals, people don't naturally have a massive or well-contoured biceps muscle. Many people build up some muscle size by doing manual labour (lifting a pick or hammer, for instance) but generally do not progress beyond a minimal development. That is because the nature of nonspecific-training is not progressive. A person lifts a heavy hammer for a day or two, gets sore and builds some muscle size. However, if this is done every day the soreness and the growth come to an end because the hammer weighs the same and the biceps ceases to respond. If a person were to use a progressively heavier hammer then he could build up increasingly larger biceps. However, that is not how it works, – except for weight training. Weight training provides the premier manner in which to enlarge and strengthen the biceps through progressive resistance and well-timed rest and recuperation.

Power and Pump

The primary manner in which to use weights to increase the muscularity of the biceps is through a combination of power and pump training. Physique champion **Lee Labrada** outlines the power side of the equation by stating "the amount of muscle growth is directly linked to the heaviest weight being used for a given number of reps."[1] **Aaron Baker** defines the pump side. "The Aaron Baker biceps building secret can be summed up in two words: *deliberate contractions.* I literally control biceps growth by controlling the speed of the movement and the flex of the muscle. Not just at the point of

Paul Dillett

complete contraction, but throughout the entire movement. Even when I use heavy weight, I control every rep. The less weight I use, the more attention I pay to control, curling the weight slowly, flexing the biceps at the top, then returning even more slowly. I actually find lighter training much more intense and difficult than heavy work."[2]

The power and pump concepts are used by the top bodybuilders to build bigger bodies and most specifically, bigger biceps. **Arnold Schwarzenegger**, the man with the huge mountain-like biceps, states that he believes "the muscles must be ***constantly pumped*** up and feel as though they have been freshly worked all day long. If there is no pump, there is no muscle growth (emphasis added)."[3] The man with the most Olympia titles, massive **Lee Haney**, points to the fact that power is the key when he says "without question, mass and power are the most important concepts in bodybuilding. That is the most categorical statement I can make about training. Definitely, the key is mass and power. The body works on supply and demand. Demand more of it physically, and your body will compensate for the poundage increas-

es by producing the amount of muscle size needed to extend the workload. That's the basic, common sense principle. That's why power movements must always be included and retained."[4]

The key to muscle growth is a combination of progressive power and pump movements. Both types of training yield results.

Form

Power and pump training are the essence for building bigger biceps. But there is one other element that must be included in this mix to make it complete – form. Good form is absolutely necessary. **Paul Dillet**, the gigantic bodybuilding champion (with 24 inch arms) points out that he may be lifting next to some little guy who is using the same amount of weight or he (Paul) may even be using less weight for curls, but there is one very important difference. Paul focuses on great form. Why? Form builds muscle.[5] A writer noted of **Craig Titus** that "his form is full and deep."[6] It is the full form that builds a full arm.

The combination of form with power or pump style training is super effective and builds awesome biceps. That is the advice from the preceding experts, and the average measurements of their arms would be around 22 inches!

How do you incorporate power, pump, and form into your biceps training program? You can use a straight power approach (super-heavy weights, more weight concentrated for 5 to 7 repetitions per set with emphasis on the movement of the weight) or a straight pump approach (lighter weight, more muscle-concentrated effort for 8 to 15 repetitions, more emphasis on the feel of the movement). Good form can and should be part of the power and pump workouts. There is more to form than just building quality muscle quicker - if your form is not good you may injure yourself and throw your training off track for quite some time. Make certain that good form is part of all your biceps training workouts.

The Mix

There is a time for strict power workouts and there is a time for pure pump workouts, but the best approach is to mix the two. There is no law which states that you have to use either approach exclusively. If you take a look at most of the routines the champions do you will find that many of them mix the pump and power approach in the same workout. **Lee Haney** does. He writes that his "technique is to begin with two power exercises and finish with rhythmic (pumping) exercises."[7] That approach is used by many of the best bodybuilders. Some use one power movement and a couple of pumping movements (per bodypart) and others use a couple of power movements mixed with a couple of pumping movements. **Aaron Baker**, a large bodybuilder with very big biceps, notes that he has "always preferred the first exercise in a workout to be the mass builder."[8] Aaron then finishes the arms off with a pump style exercise. The split approach of power and pump style in a workout is a great one for giving your biceps a full menu of stimulation. **Craig Titus** starts his training with power movements and then moves on to pump movements. "It's good to finish the workout with a nice pump and to get that blood into the muscle," says Craig.[9] Many of the top bodybuilders use a similar scheme. The workouts for your biceps outlined in *Animal Arms* will be a variety including power, pump and a mixture of both.

Building the Biceps with Intensity

Whatever style of workout you are using, it is essential that you perform it with full blown intensity. **Paul Dillet**, the man with the massive biceps, points to intensity as being a crucial factor in forming quality muscle. "When I talk about mental intensity I'm really talking about the ability to concentrate on what you're doing. It's the guy who puts the most intensity into his training who is going to get the size."[10]

To build bigger biceps you have to give your workout everything you have. Workouts that are less than all-out will maintain the biceps muscle; but to gain, to move ahead into a new level of arm development, you have to get intense. You have to pour everything you have into moving the metal for one more

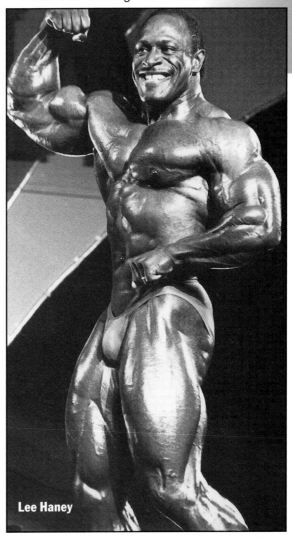

Lee Haney

repetition, even when you think you can't. It is the willingness to go to the extreme that will make your arm muscles different than the average guy. ***Muscles are built when worked at the point of extreme intensity.*** It is your job to keep your training at this level.

The Exercises

The exercises are the central element for building bigger and better biceps. Other elements play an important supporting role (diet, rest, recuperation, etc.) The biggest factor is the workout, the group of exercises used to bring about change to the biceps. The right exercises will work the specific muscle group in a designed manner for a planned effect – larger and more shapely biceps.

Achim Albrecht

The Curl

The biceps curl is the most basic, straightforward manner in which to train the biceps. The heavy curl is a rugged exercise, and it produces results. Big **Achim Albrecht** describes the curl:

"Since the prehistoric days of body-building, one question has been asked more than any other: what is the single best mass-building exercise for the biceps? My answer to that question is the same as it was in those earliest days: the regular old-fashioned standing barbell curl. Mass is built from heavy, basic compound exercises. For biceps, the standing barbell curl is the most basic and compound. That means you must not complicate the movement. The most common mistake I see is allowing the upper arms to move forward during the curl. When this happens, the anterior deltoids are worked more than the biceps, plus, the barbell is displaced from the power plane, preventing the biceps from being fully fatigued from the set."[11]

Achim goes on to note that many bodybuilders make the mistake of using a grip that is too narrow. He suggests a shoulder width grip for the most effective and powerful curling. He also points out the necessity of getting a full extension and contraction.

Standing barbell curls, are most effective when they are performed with a heavy weight. That does not mean using cheating or sloppy form. **Paul Dillett** notes "for mass, nothing beats the old standbys of basic heavy barbell and dumbell curls. When I say heavy, it's relative. Heavy does not mean piling on so much weight that you have to break form just to complete a rep."[12] Heavy curls are to be done in good form, letting the arms rather than the momentum of the action raise the weight. You are training your arm muscles, not your thigh and back muscles.

For putting on muscle size, the regular curl, performed with heavy weights in good form, is the ultimate arm mass movement.

The curl movement is also the most basic biceps training exercise of all. It is the best size producer for most people,

Bertil Fox

The Hammer Curl

The hammer curl is an exercise you often see mixed in with a champion bodybuilder's routine. Why? The hammer curl is very effective for adding height and mass to the biceps muscle. It does so in an indirect manner, but with direct results.

The hammer curl works on the brachialis muscle. The brachialis muscle is a flat and broad muscle that is spread out on the arm and lies between the humerus (upper arm bone) and the biceps muscle. Technically the hammer curl does not work the biceps muscles but the muscles that lie just below the biceps. **Bertil Fox**, a bodybuilding champion known for his incredibly massive and dense arms, points out that "anyone who neglects brachialis development automatically limits the height and ultimate mass of his biceps, because a well-developed brachialis will push the biceps upward away from the humerus and give the biceps more apparent height and mass."[14]

but it is not the only exercise for building the biceps. **Arnold Schwarzenegger** noted:

"I believe all exercises are effective. Some arm movements work better for one bodybuilder than for another, that is true. Barbell curls may be wonderful for building the biceps, but then who says seated dumbell curls with heavy weights are not more effective? They might be, for you, and the only way you'll find out is to experiment."[13]

Use the regular barbell curl and make it the centerpiece of your biceps-training routine, especially in the initial stages. It will produce results. But there are other excellent biceps exercises besides the basic barbell curl. One of these is the hammer curl.

There are several exercises that work the brachialis including the reverse curl, the zottman curl, and the hammer curl. **Bertil's** favorite exercise for brachialis development is the seated incline dumbell hammer curl. "It's a normal incline dumbell curl performed with the palms facing inward toward each other throughout the entire movement, from a straight-armed position to one in which the arms are fully flexed."[15] The hammer curl is so called because it looks like you are swinging a hammer when you lift the dumbell. When the palms are facing in toward each other instead of up or down, the angle of the wrist places the workload on the brachialis muscle. At the top of the movement,

Flex Wheeler, Michael Francois and Charles Clairmonte

straighten the hands so that the brachialis doesn't get an opportunity to rest. This puts continual pressure on the brachialis and stimulates quicker growth.

The hammer curl is more effective when performed on an incline bench. In fact, almost any dumbell exercise is more effective when performed in an inclined manner because the incline allows for a further stretch and this gives the muscle more stimulation. Using the incline bench you go beyond the point where you would normally stop the exercise and get a deeper extension and longer contraction. This is more difficult, but produces a larger, fuller muscle.

For an even better action on the incline hammer curl, place your feet on another bench. This action will tilt your body just right for a total stretch and enable the greatest possible development.

For super arm size, maximize the development of the brachialis muscle!

The growth of the brachialis muscle is crucial for getting the ultimate potential from your biceps. As **Bertil** mentioned, the brachialis, when fully developed, pushes the biceps muscle up and out.

When you have significantly trained the brachialis muscle you have in effect doubled the development of the upper arm. The biceps will be built up, and so will the brachialis muscle. This dual development will really give your arms muscular size and shape.

One bodybuilder who had a very dense side development of the brachialis muscle was **Arnold Schwarzenegger**. His upper arm has a very large mound of knotted muscle on the side where the brachialis was pushing the biceps not only upward but outward. This unique shape is the result of a lot of hammer, reverse curl, and zottman work. The hammer curl and similar exercises also build up the large muscles of the forearm. The hammer curl is an essential movement if you want to fully develop your arm potential and an absolute necessity for biceps density.

The Preacher Curl

Another essential movement for building awesome biceps is the preacher curl. The preacher curl is so named because the exercise resembles a preacher leaning over his pulpit preaching a sermon. It also goes by the name "Scott curl," named after the first Mr. Olympia, **Larry Scott**, who often used the preacher curl to develop his massive and full arms.

This curl is performed with a special attachment on the bench. This is a board that is covered with foam or some other element to make the hardness less noticeable. The board is angled down at a 30- 45- or 60-degree slope, or is straight down. The backside of the arms are placed on the bench. This ensures that they remain stable and do not move at all. One of the key functions of the preacher bench is to ensure isolation of the biceps muscle. The angle of the preacher curl points all of the action directly on the biceps. Most curling motions involve some assistance from other muscle groups, even when you are trying to avoid such assistance. The preacher curl, by specific design, takes all of that help away. For this reason, you have to use lighter weights with the preacher curl, but the exercise brings better results.

It is important to follow pure form in the preacher curl. The very man-

ner of the exercise forces a purity of motion, but you must be careful to lower the bar slowly in the downward extension. If you don't, if you bounce the bar, you can severely injure your biceps. One bodybuilder tore his biceps out severely by not heeding this warning and inflicted a painful and unnecessary injury upon himself.

Another key aspect of maximizing the motion and effectiveness of the preacher curl is to not let the arms rest at the top of the movement (where there is the opportunity and temptation to take it easy for a second or two) but rather to deliberately and forcefully contract the biceps muscles at the top of the lift. Squeeze the biceps as hard as you can, then lower the bar back down again. To make the most of the preacher curl, you need to concentrate heavily

The preacher curl, as performed by Larry Scott.

on every repetition of every set that you are doing.

The preacher curl is one of the very best exercises for building awesome arms!

Use the preacher curl often throughout your arm training routine. Don't stray too far

from this excellent biceps building exercise. You can use it with either a barbell or dumbells.

The preacher curl can be used with either a pump or power approach, although the movement lends itself more to the pump style of training. **Robby Robinson**, a champion bodybuilder known for his super-awesome arms, often uses the preacher curls and combines a power movement with the pump. He says "this is a superb mass builder for the biceps because you get a maximum contraction on every rep. I always use maximum weight to get maximal growth stimulation. I also always allow the weights to travel as far as possible so that the biceps are fully stretched. I maintain tension on the biceps at all times, even when the weights are at shoulder level. I lower the weights slowly in a controlled manner on every rep."[16]

If you want to get an awesome pair of arms, incorporate the preacher curl into your workout. You can use a barbell or a dumbell. And try the different angles of the preacher curl. The preacher curl bench with a straight drop (90 degree angle) places the emphasis of the lift on the upper biceps. The preacher curl bench with more of a slope (approximately 45 degree angle) places more of the emphasis of the lift on the lower biceps. Use both for full development.

The preacher curl is fantastic because it allows you to put all of your energy on just the motion of the lift and takes away any momentum that would help you do the lift. Thus, making your biceps muscles do all of the work. This exercise is so fantastic that it was one of the only exercises **Larry Scott** did. He performed the preacher curl in a variety of manners, and it worked wonders for him. He developed a pair of the fullest biceps muscles ever seen. **Larry Scott**'s biceps inspired big **Lou Ferrigno** in his arm training.[17] And it was primarily the preacher curl that built Lou's famous biceps. If you want awesome biceps, make certain the preacher curl is often included in your various biceps workouts.

Dumbell Concentration Curl

Another essential training tool for building tremendous biceps is the dumbell concentration curl. This movement is a favorite

Robby Robinson

of all the top bodybuilders. In *Pumping Iron* **Arnold Schwarzenegger** is seen pumping out repetition after repetition of the dumbell concentration curl as his biceps swell to gigantic proportions. **Robby Robinson,** who built 20.5 inch arms at a bodyweight of just 207, also favors this exercise. **Robby** states that the dumbell concentration curl "Allows you to fully control the action of the biceps."[18] **Robby** keeps the tension on the biceps throughout the motion. **Aaron Baker** also uses the dumbell concentration curl often. He braces his arm against his inner thigh as he sits on a bench (as opposed to the version Arnold used in *Pumping Iron* of a bent-over position with a swinging arm) and squeezes the muscles at the top of the movement.[19]

You can perform the dumbell concentration curl in either a seated or standing position. The seated position is somewhat better in that it allows for more concentration on the specific move. Grasp a dumbell and sit on a bench. Slowly and deliberately curl the dumbell all the way to full contraction (this will put the dumbell up near your chin). Lower the dumbell all the way back down in a slow, smooth extension. Experiment with the angles that you use as you bring the dumbell up. You may find a particular angle that really works well for you. **Albert Beckles**, a man with massive biceps advises you to "train the arms from every possible angle."[20] Use the dumbell concentration curl at an angle which hits the biceps the hardest. Also use the inner part of your thigh to keep your upper arm steady and straight so that the biceps does all of the work during the exercise.

The dumbell concentration curl is a good move for forcing out some repetitions in the growth zone. Use a dumbell that is heavy enough to make the last three repetitions pure torture. Push yourself as hard as possible. Remember that the mind fails before the body does, so don't let the pain barrier intimidate you and keep you from a pair of awesome arms.

Start

Bertil Fox builds his world-class biceps with dumbell concentration curls.

Finish

Larry Scott flexes his biceps for a young admirer.

The Cheat Curl

There is always an exception to the rule, an aberration to the normal flow of events. The cheat curl is just such an animal. The general principle for training the biceps is to perform the exercises (which are mainly curls) in the strictest manner possible, with a very pure form – which means no cheating. The exception to this rule is the cheat curl. The cheat curl is a curl performed with heavier weights with which you deliberately cheat the weight up. The reason for doing this is to shock the biceps with the heavier weight and to accustom your mind and body to a "heavy duty" approach. The important factor in the cheat curl is to not let your body get out of line as you "cheat" the weight upwards. To cheat the weight up you give it an extra boost with the thighs and also use momentum as a help. Some people use this style all of the time and obtain few, if any results. But this movement works well as a temporary shocking motion. You would use a cheat curl occasionally to jolt your arms with the heavy weight but would not use it beyond that.

The best exercise manner for the cheat curl is the regular heavy barbell movement. When you use this movement make certain you use heavier weights; using your previous weight amount will not produce any results. You need to go heavy – real heavy. **Arnold** would use over 250 pounds for cheat curls!

Cheating and Shock Principles

It is necessary to occasionally cheat and/or shock the muscles to prevent them from lapsing into a rut. A routine can cause boredom and stall the training progress and muscle growth if it is used exclusively. When this happens you can apply exceptions to the rules and experiment with some new ideas for building bigger biceps. It is essential to try out new concepts. For instance, a workout should consist of fewer sets with more intensity; but that is a general rule, not an absolute. In fact, the man to first break the 21-inch arm barrier **Leroy Colbert**, noted that for quite some time he worked his biceps according to the expert advice of only three sets

Some trainers advise starting the dumbell concentration curl with the weaker arm to prioritize the effect of the initial burst of training. Make the dumbell concentration curl an essential element of your biceps building program. Use it at the end of your workout to "top off" a great routine. Or use it at the start of a routine as a pre exhaust movement before heavy barbell curls.

Super Tip – When using the dumbell concentration curl, after you have performed as many repetitions as possible with the weight, pump out a couple more repetitions with the assistance of your free arm. Put just enough pressure on the upward stroke to enable you to pull in 1 or 2 more repetitions.

per biceps workout. It was only when he began to experiment with more sets (he got up to 15 sets per biceps workout) that his arms really started to take off. Some people thrive on a biceps workout that consists of many sets. **Dr. Ollie McClay** uses multiple sets of the various biceps curl movements. His arms remain over 21-inches and he is over 50-years old. Don't work out with your head in the sand – try different approaches to building your biceps. Experiment with every factor in the muscle size/shape equation. Multiple sets, repetitions, cheating and shock movements may work well for you; or they might not work at all. The best way to find out is to use a certain specific approach for a cycle and see if it works or not. The best time to try a new idea is during a new training cycle.

Achim Albrect is a bodybuilding champion who uses shock training to stir up his growth gains. His definition of a shock workout sums it all up pretty well. He says "whereas under normal circumstances I keep my reps in the 6 to 10 range, with a lighter weight I can do sets of 20, 30 and sometimes 50. But just because the amount of weight doesn't impress anyone doesn' t mean I don't feel any soreness. In fact, this training style is a killer. I end up fighting to complete 10 to 15 more reps even after the burning sensation has begun to inflame my muscles, but I keep pumping out the reps anyway. Not fast and jerky reps, mind you – I do them in a smooth, restrained fashion, controlling the muscle completely with my mind, and really feeling it work. Do it right and you'll definitely feel sore the next day. This shock

ANIMAL ARMS TWO

Lee Priest

Start

Finish

Alternate dumbell curls are a regular exercise in Jamo Nezzar's biceps routine.

routine, done on an occasional basis, can provide the physical and mental stimulation your body needs."

Alternating Dumbell Curls

The alternating dumbell curl can be performed from a seated or standing position. The alternating sequence allows you to focus on just the arm being trained instead of having to curl both arms at the same time. The best seated version of the alternating curl is performed on an incline bench for maximum stretch and growth. You can load up and go fairly heavy in the standing version of the alternating dumbell curl. This exercise is a great one to perform supination motions with. Supination occurs when you turn your wrist as you lift the weight. This is not really possible with a barbell (although there is a specialty barbell that allows you do to so) but works with a dumbell. Supination, the turning of the wrist as you raise the dumbell, works the

biceps more directly. **Arnold Schwarzenegger** was a big believer in supination techniques for deeper development of the biceps.
Super Tip: For further biceps development, utilize some supination movements with dumbells.

Reverse Curl

The reverse curl is a movement that primarily works the brachialis muscle and also has a growth producing effect on the upper part of the forearm muscles. The reverse curl is performed with the palms of the hands facing outward instead of inward as with the regular curl. The reverse curl is particularly effective if performed on a preacher bench. The best hand placement is a little narrower than shoulder width, although you might want to experiment to find the exact best spot for your arms.

For the reverse curl, the more strict the motion, the better the result you will receive. Swinging the weight up in this move is not really effective at all. Intense concentration is also necessary for maximum results. A couple of sets of the reverse curl will pump up the brachialis and have your biceps bulging. You can perform the reverse curl with a cable pulley system also.

EZ-Curl

A variation of the curl is the"e-z curl." This is a curl performed on a shorter bar that has been variously bent to allow the biceps to be trained at different angles, and to take much of the strain off the wrists. Some people really like the ez-curl; others find it does not do as much for them as a straight bar. Experiment with it and find out if it is better than the straight bar for your arms. Try each of the various angles.

Close-Grip Curl

The close-grip curl is just that – a barbell curl performed with the hands 5 to 10 inches apart. The placement of the hands affects the biceps differently than it does with the regular curl. As with the e-z curl, give the close-grip curl a whirl to find out if it has a positive effect on your biceps.

Cable Curl

One of the more popular versions of curling is the cable curl. The cable curl is effective because it keeps continuous tension on the biceps. The cable curl can be used with both arms (similar to the barbell curl) or with an attachment that enables the curl to be performed with one arm (similar to a dumbell curl). The cable curl can also be used with a preacher-bench-style curl or a reverse curl. The cable curl is used by most of the top bodybuilders. **Vince Taylor** uses many cable curling movements to train his large biceps.

Lateral Curl

The lateral curl is performed with the dumbells on an incline bench. Bring the dumbells up to your shoulders, then lower them out and down to the side. This is different from the regular path of the curl, which would travel along

the length of the body down to the thighs. Instead, the lateral curl moves out and away from the body, with the dumbell never going below the waist. This is a good exercise for separating the biceps muscle from the triceps muscle on the inside of the arm.

Another version of this lateral curling motion can be done with a cable curl if you

Finish

Boston's Mike Matarazzo performs one-arm cable curls.

Start

Ronnie Coleman

have access to a double cable curling unit with a high pulley. Grasp the cable handles and curl your arm in toward your head, contract the biceps muscles hard for a two-count, then return the cable to a full side extension, and repeat.

Close Grip Chinup

What do you do if you are somewhere where there are no weights available? Perhaps you are on vacation or on a business trip and do not have ready access to a gym – what do you do for your biceps? An excellent free-hand exercise is the close grip chinup. This great exercise utilizes your bodyweight and gives the biceps a challenging workout. Of course if you wish to advance in muscle growth beyond an initial spurt, you will have to strap a weight to your body. But the close grip chinup is a good exercise to use in a jam when you are caught away from the weights.

21's

Twenty-one's are also called the three part curl. This exercise is great for shocking some growth into the arms. Pick up a barbell (although it can also be done with a dumbell) and curl the weight from the thighs **but only up to the half-way point of a normal curl** (around the midsection). Perform seven of these half motions, then perform seven repetitions in the opposite manner, from the mind-point of the curl up to the finishing point. Finally, perform seven repetitions of a full curling motion. As you can figure, the three parts add up to 21 repetitions, hence the name. Make certain that all three parts are performed without any rest. This is a shock movement which will really stimulate the biceps.

The Rack

Another exercise used for shocking the arm muscles into growth is the "the rack." This is not a medieval torture device, although you might think so after you try it. The rack is so-named for taking the various weights in a barbell or dumbell rack and curling each one consecutively. You might start with a pair of 10-pound dumbells and work up to a pair of 50-pound dumbells, or start with a 50-pound barbell and work up to a 120-pound barbell. You perform several repetitions with each weight, move on to the next heavier weight, and rotate back to the beginning after you have moved through all the weights designated for that workout. This type of routine is quite brutal but will force some new muscle size onto the arms. Use it only occasionally when you have a little extra spunk.

Sergio Oliva

Putting it all together

These are a few of the best of the biceps building exercises that will provide you with plenty of stimulation for *animal arms*. Of course, how you use them in a workout is crucial. At the end of this chapter there is a section devoted to the specific use of these exercises in different routines. Additionally, the biceps routines of the top bodybuilders are also included. As you look through the various routines, notice which exercises are used most frequently. There is a reason why some of these exercises are used again and again by the different champions

– it is because those are the biceps exercises that work. Use many biceps exercises in your routine. Check out the *Biceps Addendum* for action-packed arms workouts and then build your own biceps approach so that you too can have *animal arms*.

1. Greg Zulak, "Lee Labrada Biceps," *MuscleMag International.* May/June 1991, p. 138
2. Aaron Baker, "Deliberate Contractions," *Flex*, August 1990, pp. 63-64
3. Arnold Schwarzenegger in the 1969 edition of *Muscle Builder/Power*
4. Lee Haney, "Big, Bigger, Best!" *Flex*, August 1990, p. 44
5. Paul Dillett, "24 Inches of Monster Meat," *Flex*, August 1992, p. 140
6. Greg Zulak, "Craig Titus's Titan Workouts for Terrific Triceps," *MuscleMag International,* April 1995, p. 168
7. Lee Haney, p. 44
8. T.C. Luoma, "Armed Warfare," *MuscleMag International*, May/June 1991, p. 118
9. Greg Zulak, p. 168
10. Paul Dillett, p. 140
11.Achim Albrecht, "Stand Bi Your Curls," *Flex*, August 1992, p. 185
12. Paul Dillett, p. 140
13. Arnold Schwarzenegger in the May 1979 issue of *Muscle & Fitness*
14. Bertil Fox, "Mountains from Molehills," *Flex*, August 1990, p. 18
15. Ibid
16. Gene Mozee, "Mass from the Past," *Ironman*, October 1994, p. 144
17. Lou Ferrigno and Douglas Kent Hall, "The Incredible Lou Ferrigno," (New York: Simon and Schuster, 1982) p. 28
18. Ibid
19. Aaron Baker, pp. 63-64
20. Albert Beckles, "Three Rules of Arms," *Flex*, November 1995, p33.

Achim Albrecht

Biceps Addendum

Basic Biceps Workout
Barbell curls
3 x 8-10 repetitions
Alternate dumbell curls
3 x 8-10 repetitions
Concentration curls
3 x 8-12 repetitions

Bulk Biceps Workout
Barbell curls, heavy
3 x 6-10 repetitions
Cheat curls, heavy
2 x 5-7 repetitions
Concentration curls, heavy
3 x 6-8 repetitions
Reverse curls, heavy
2 x 6-8 repetitions

Power/Pump Combo Workout
Barbell curls
3 x 6-10 repetitions
Preacher curls
3 x 8-12 repetitions
Hammer curls
2 x 8-12 repetitions
Cable curls, heavy
2 x 5-7 repetitions

Shock Routine
Perform 1 set of all out high intensity preacher barbell curls every hour for 8-10 hours. Rest for the full hour after each set, then repeat on the hour. Aim for a range of 10-15 repetitions; lighten the load toward the end of the day.

Biceps Blowout Workout
Barbell curls
4 x 6-10 repetitions
Preacher curls
4 x 6-10 repetitions
Hammer curls
4 x 8-10 repetitions
Dumbell concentration curls
4 x 8-10 repetitions

Peak Contraction Workout
Preacher curls
3 x 8-12 repetitions
Dumbell concentration curls
3 x 8-12 repetitions
Barbell curls, light
2 x 15 repetitions

Flex Wheeler

Brachialis Specialization Workout

Reverse preacher curls
3 x 8-12 repetitions
Incline hammer curls
3 x 10-15 repetitions

Cable Curl Workout

Standing cable curls
4 x 8-10 repetitions
One-arm cable curls
3 x 8-10 repetitions
Preacher cable curls
3 x 6-10 repetitions

Heavy-Duty Super Intensity Workout

Preacher curls slow motion
1-2 x 6-10 repetitions
Machine curls slow motion
1 x 6-10 repetitions

Try some of these various workouts for a cycle and find out which one's work for your biceps. Or mix and match to meet your specific biceps-training needs. There is no law that confines you to one specific type of routine or sequence of biceps exercises. As you use the various biceps exercises you will discover that some exercises really work wonders. Make these a main part of your future biceps-training routines, but always remain open-minded and willing to try something new.

Remember the keys to building awesome biceps:

Form: As strict as possible – full extensions and contractions
Intensity: As hard as you can in good form.
Variety: Change the workout to stimulate the biceps and provoke new growth.
Pump & power: Mix these two crucial components in equal amounts.
Deliberate contractions: "Feel" the muscle work and squeeze it tight at the top.
Pushing past the pain barrier: Get those extra repetitions that are so very important for stimulating new growth.

Super Tip 1: Rent *Pumping Iron* and watch the squat routine with Arnold Schwarzenegger and Ed Corney. Watch as Arnold has Ed forcefully move past the pain barrier and into the growth zone. Listen carefully as Arnold explains how to get those extra repetitions that bring growth. Apply this concept to your biceps-training and they will grow gigantic.

Super Tip 2: Always "lay-out" the barbell or dumbell you are curling to get a deeper stretch and fuller growth. This means fully extending your arms until they lay-out and are locked out at the downward stroke of the motion. The only exception to this lay-out rule is when you are performing cheat curls.

Bodybuilding Champions' Biceps Routines

Robby Robinson

Robby won more than 300 trophies before turning pro. He is well known for super arms with great size and shape. Robby often won the "Night of the Champions." His arms remain incredible after decades of competition and he won the first Masters Mr. Olympia. Gene Mozee measured Robby's arms at 20.5 inches cold (no pump) at a bodyweight of only 207, an incredible arm size for that weight.[1] Robby's biceps are one of his trademarks.

Sergio Oliva

Robby's biceps workout:
Barbell curls 4 x 8, 8, 6, 4-6
Preacher curls 4 x 8, 8, 6, 4-6
Dumbell concentration curls 4 x 8

Sergio Oliva
Sergio is another bodybuilder who has tremen-dous arm size at a fairly light body weight. Sergio's arms are reportedly larger than his head.

Sergio Oliva's biceps workout:²
Reverse curls
6 x 15 repetitions
Cheat curls
6 x 10-12 repetitions
Scott bench curls
5 x 10-12 repetitions + five more sets at a lighter weight
Dumbell curls
10 x 10 repetitions

Nasser El Sonbaty flexes his monstrous biceps onstage.

Larry Scott
Larry Scott's biceps are so famous that their development produced a name for an exercise and a bench. Larry's biceps inspired many body-builders to develop larger arms, including Lou Ferrigno. Larry's biceps are perhaps the fullest biceps that have been developed.

Larry Scott's biceps workout:³
tri-set
Preacher (Scott) dumbell curls
4 x 6
Preacher (Scott) barbell curls
4 x 6
Preacher (Scott) reverse curls
4 x 6
Steeper-angle preacher curls
3-4 x 6

Michael Francois

Michael is a powerful bodybuilder rising to the top of the current bodybuilding scene. He is the 1995 Schwarzenegger Classic champion. He trains his biceps every 10 days to allow for adequate recuperation from his heavy duty workouts.

Michael Francios biceps workout:[4]

Heavy barbell curls
3 x 8-12
One-arm preacher curls
3 x 8-12
Cable concentration curls
3 x 8-12

Vince Taylor

Vince Taylor is another guy with great big guns. Vince is somewhat unusual in that he likes to use cables instead of barbells and dumbells to train his biceps. However unusual, it must be working because he has tremendous arms.

Vince Taylor's biceps workout:[5]

Reverse one-arm cable biceps curls
4-5 sets of 6-12 repetitions
Cable concentration curls
4-5 sets of 6-12 repetitions
Single-arm hammer cable curls
5 sets of 6-12 repetitions

Arnold Schwarzenegger

Arnold – the name alone brings to mind the vision of a massive biceps, rugged as the mountains where Arnold came from. Arnold's massive 22.5 inch biceps became the symbol of bodybuilding for the past several decades. Arnold took his arms over 20 inches by the time he was around 20 years of age, then added more mass and refinement. Arnold's biceps are truly awesome.

Arnold's biceps routine:[6]

Barbell cheat curls
6-7 sets of 6-8 repetitions
Sitting dumbell curls
6-7 sets of 6-8 repetitions
Preacher (Scott) curls
6-7 sets of 6-8 repetitions

Michael Francois

Lee Haney

Another Mr. Olympia who had 22+ inch arms is massive Lee Haney. Lee held the Mr. O title longer than anyone, and his big biceps were one of the reasons why.

Lee Haney's biceps routine:[7]

Monday
Barbell curls
5 sets of 8-10 repetitions
Incline dumbell curls
5 sets of 6-8 repetitions
Barbell preacher curls
5 sets of 8-10 repetitions

Thursday
Standing dumbell curls
5 sets of 6-8 repetitions
Barbell preacher curls
5 sets of 8-10 repetitions
Dumbell concentration curls
5 sets of 10-12 repetitions

Lee Priest

Saturday
Dumbell concentration curls
5 sets of 10-12 repetitions
Cable curls
5 sets of 6-8 repetitions

Lee Labrada

Lee Labrada is one of the top bodybuilders who almost took the Olympia title on several occasions. Although not as big as some of the behemoths, he was able to handle the monsters partly due to his fantastic biceps.

Lee Labrada's biceps routine:[8]
One-arm concentration curls
1 x 6-8, 1 x 10, 1 x 10
Barbell or preacher curls
1 x 6-8, 1 x 10, 1 x 10
Alternate dumbell curls
1 x 6-8, 1 x 10

Sonny Schmidt

Sonny is massive and a very powerful champion (5'10", 280+ pounds) who recently won the Masters Mr. Olympia. He is in such great condition that he can pass for being 10 years younger than he really is and competes in both the open and masters competitions (he did great on the European Grand Prix tour after winning the Master's Olympia).

Sonny Schmidt's biceps workout:[9]
Barbell curls
5 x 10-15 repetitions
Preacher curls
5 x 10-15 repetitions
Concentration curls
5 x 10-15 repetitions

Dorian Yates

Dorian is the current Mr. Olympia and an extremely intense bodybuilder. He injured one of his large biceps some time ago, but it has recovered well and looked good enough for him to win his fourth consecutive Mr. O title. Dorian uses superhigh intensity workouts for his arms with a very low set range.

Dorian Yates' biceps workout:[10]

Seated incline dumbell curls
1 x 6-8 repetitions
Concentration curls
1 x 6-8 repetitions
Barbell curls
1 x 6-8 repetitions
Hammer curls
1 x 6-8 repetitions

Jason Marcovici

Jason is known for his big biceps. He has performed cheat curls with 250 pounds and alternate dumbell curls with 100 pound dumbells. He has a couple of different workouts he uses for his biceps.

Jason Marcovici's biceps workout:[11]

Workout 1
Alternate incline dumbell curls
4 x 6-10 repetitions
One-arm cable curls
3 x 6-8 repetitions
        or
Barbell preacher curls
3 x 6-8 repetitions

Workout 2
Barbell curls
4 x 6-8 repetitions
One-arm concentration curls
3 x 8-12 repetitions
Machine preacher curls
3 x 8-12 repetitions
plus an occasional few sets of hammer curls.

Rick Valente

Rick is the star of *Bodyshaping* and a former competitive bodybuilder. His favorite bodypart to train is his arms.

Rick Valente's biceps workout:

Barbell curls
3-5 x 6-8 repetitions, 1 x 35
Seated dumbell curls
3-5 x 6-8 repetitions, 1 x 35
Preacher curls
3-5 x 6-8 repetitions, 1 x 35

As you look through these various workouts, notice what exercises the champions are using. You should consider trying those biceps exercises that show up most frequently. And also remember that you might not need quite as many sets per exercise as some of the champions. Check out the different workouts and find those that work best for building awesome biceps that make up one part of *Animal Arms*.

Paul Dillett

1. Gene Mozee, "Mass from Past," *Ironman*, October 1994, pp. 142-145
2. John Little, "Guns from Olympus," *Flex*, January 1993, p. 23
3. Ibid
4. Mike Francois, "Ungodly Guns," *Flex*, January 1996, p. 62
5. Reg Bradford, "Huge, Massive, Freaky Arm Routine," *Muscular Development*
6. John Little, "Guns from Olympus," *Flex*, January 1993, p.23
7. Ibid., p. 29
8. Greg Zulak, "Lee Labrada's Biceps," *MuscleMag International*, May-June 1991, p. 140
9. Marty Gallagher, "Sonny Schmidt, How He Won the Masters Olympia," *Muscle & Fitness*, January 1996, p. 86
10. Bill Geiger and Dorian Yates, "How I won the Mr. Olympia," *Muscle & Fitness*, January 1996, p. 76
11. Greg Zulak, "Massive Marcovici," *MuscleMag International*, August 1994, p. 66

Lee Priest

Chapter Three

The biceps are the show muscles of the arm, as mentioned in the last chapter. Everyone is concerned about the build of the biceps, and rightly so. The biceps are an impressive muscle. They provide the mountain-type of raise in the appearance of the arm. But in reality, the biceps are not even the most important muscle on the upper arm. That distinction goes to the triceps. The triceps are one of the most overlooked and underrated muscles on the body. One of the most common and devastating mistakes novice body-builders make is overlooking the tremendous importance of the triceps muscle in the scheme

Flex Wheeler

The Triceps: True Source of Arm Strength and Size

of overall arm size. The primary reason this error is so bad is that *the key to arm size is the triceps!* If you want massive and muscular arms, you cannot afford to overlook the triceps. In fact, you cannot even afford to just break even – you have to place a real emphasis on training the triceps if you have any hopes of making your arms massive. It needs to be repeated several times – the key to real arm size is found in developing the triceps muscles. It is not the biceps, but the triceps that provide the size for the arm. If you want massive and muscular arms, you must build the triceps muscles to a high degree of development.

It takes a lot of discipline to set aside the desire to spend more training time on the biceps, and get into triceps training. But it is essential if you want "hot" arms.

Why are the triceps the key to mighty arm muscle? The triceps are the key to massive upper arm size because the triceps muscle comprises approximately 66 percent of the upper arm. The biceps muscles only make up about one-third of the size of the upper arm yet that is where most people spend all of their arm training effort. They camp on the 33 percent of the arm that the biceps affects and overlook the 66 percent of the arm that the triceps affects. It is no wonder that they do not have large arm measurements if the majority of their time is spent on training the biceps.

Mike Christian

To build big arms, focus on training the triceps. The triceps comprise approximately 66% of the muscle size of the upper arm. The bigger your triceps, the bigger your arms!

If you want bigger arms, it is silly to spend all of your arm training effort on the biceps. Make triceps-training a priority and watch your arm size increase.

Triceps overview

The triceps is composed of three muscles with a common tendinous attachment - hence the name triceps. The long head arises from a tendon on the scapula; the lateral from the posterior surface of the upper-arm (humerus) bone; and the medial head has its origin in an area just below that of the lateral head. All three insert into a single tendon attached to the forearm. The action of the triceps is to extend the forearm, with the long head also aiding in bringing the arm closer to the body from a lateral position.[1]

The primary manner in which to train the triceps is through a pushing motion. Generally, any pushing motion with the upper body will involve the triceps, particularly when performed with a narrow grip. Triceps training can be part of compound work (where the triceps play an important but often secondary role such as with the bench press or shoulder press) or isolation work where the triceps are the central focus (involving exercises such as the triceps cable pushdown or dumbell kickback).

The triceps can grow impressively in both size and strength. The three muscles of the triceps combine together to provide a powerful pushing force. The triceps are one of the more essential muscle groups, especially for the upper torso. The triceps are more involved in the many movements of the body than are the biceps muscles.

When fully developed, the triceps are an awesome looking muscle group. When flexed and contracted, they form a large horseshoe shape on the back of the upper arm. Rigid, sharp lines form like a mountain ridge as the triceps muscles are tightened. The triceps muscles also make the biceps muscles look better as they add that awesome size to the underneath of the arm and give the arm shape from both the top and bottom. If you are concerned about the size measurement of your arm, you must add triceps

size to have any hope of a decent measurement. Since the triceps make up about 66 percent of the arm, adding more triceps size will greatly increase your arm measurement.

The Triceps Exercises

There are a variety of excellent exercises that provide the triceps muscles with stimulation for growing larger, stronger and more muscular. The best of these exercises will be included in the *Animal Arms* program so that you can maximize your triceps development. Try each of the various movements; they will be included in a variety of triceps training routines at the end of the chapter.

The Triceps Bench Press

The triceps bench press is one of the most basic of all the triceps training exercises. The triceps bench press is also called the close-grip bench press. That is an accurate description of this movement. The exercise is performed like a bench press, only with a very close grip. From a prone position on a bench, the barbell is lifted off the rack and the weight is lowered to a

Lee Labrada, Lee Haney and Gary Strydom

point slightly above the nipples, with the hands placed about six to fourteen inches apart. This narrow grip puts the emphasis of the stress on the triceps muscles. It is best to get a full extension and to lower the bar back down to where it touches the upper chest region, then repeat. For best results it is better to bring the bar slightly forward (to an area above the neck) as it travels upward to the top of the movement. The triceps bench press is great for building mass.

The Dip

The dip is the classic of all triceps movements and an ancient exercise. The dip builds tremendous triceps but only under a couple of conditions. First, the dip must be per-

Craig Titus

formed in the right manner. You must have the hands placed close together (narrow-grip dip), and the chin and chest must be up and out during the motion. (A wide dip with the head and chest down primarily works the outer chest.) The other condition is that you must graduate from the basic dip movement to a weighted dip after you can perform 20 non-stop repetitions in the dip. The dip is a great move for building the triceps, but only to a point. After your body has become accustomed to using your bodyweight for the dip, you cease to get any further gains unless you either increase the repetitions or increase the weight that your body is dipping with. You can increase the repetition range endlessly, but it loses its muscle-building effect once you start to get out beyond 20 or 30 repetitions and then it becomes a stamina/endurance workout. For further muscle size gains you need to add weight once you can handle 20 to 30 repetitions in the dip. When you add to your bodyweight you give your triceps a new challenge. You can do this by using a dipping belt and attaching a dumbell. Graduate the weight that you use as you maximize the target repetition range (10 to 20 repetitions maximum). This incremental increase will gradually acclimate your muscles and force larger and stronger triceps to develop. One of the side-benefits is that your ability to handle a heavy bench press or shoulder press movement will increase drastically. The dip, especially when used with weights attached to your body, will build massive arm size. One person noted that if you want big triceps, "go for parallel bar dips. When you can do 20 reps with a 100-pound dumbell hanging from your waist, you'll have 'em."[2]

The dip is performed by taking the narrow grip position, and from a full extension, dipping between the bars as far as you can go down. It is very important to move slowly into this position to avoid injuring your body. You can push upward in a powerful motion, but make certain that the downstroke is slow and controlled. Get a full extension so that the triceps muscles "lock" at the top of the dip

Lee Labrada

way through the pain barrier on this exercise is tough but pays great dividends. Push through the pain barrier and get several repetitions in the "growth zone" of the weighted dip. All of your pushing movements will become easier if you master the weighted dip and your triceps will become quite massive and powerful.

Super Tip: If you want to develop awesome size and impressive strength in your triceps, perform the weighted dip often.

The Triceps Prone Press

One of the most popular and effective triceps exercises is the triceps prone press. The triceps prone press is performed from a prone position on a bench, with a barbell held above the neck and the arms fully extended upward. A narrow grip should be employed (hands approximately six inches apart). Slowly lower the barbell until it almost touches the forehead, then press back upward in a smooth, slow motion. It is vitally important to keep the elbows in tight throughout the full movement. If you let the elbows flare out you take some of the emphasis off of the triceps (placing it more on other muscle groups) and hinder your progress in building the triceps muscles.

Keep your elbows in tight during the full motion of the triceps prone press for maximum triceps development and quicker results

movement. Make certain to go all of the way down even in the latter repetitions. There is a tendency to start cheating when the dip motion starts to cause your muscles to burn. Avoid this mistake and focus on performing the dip in good form throughout the full movement. Fighting your

Dr. Ollie McClay, a man with massive triceps, has devised a way to teach those he trains how to keep the elbows tight. He makes the person performing the triceps prone press

Ian Harrison, Lee Labrada and the late Andreas Munzer

put a weight belt around their arms to prevent them from flaring their elbows outward. A few sessions using this method teaches a person to keep their elbows in during the motion of the triceps prone press.

It is also very important to make the triceps prone press a motion performed under strict control. This exercise is not referred to as the "skull-crusher" for nothing! You cannot afford to let the bar drop when it is suspended directly above your forehead or your lifting days will be over. So go slow and keep the weight under control throughout the movement.

The triceps prone press is fantastic for putting direct pressure on the triceps muscle group and causing muscle size and shape growth. Lock the triceps very briefly at the top of the movement on every second or third repetition. Do not lock out on every repetition.

To lock or not to lock.

Should you lock out the movement when training with weights (locking out is performing a full extension to the point of going as far as you can and "locking" the arms into

position at that point). One bodybuilding writer notes that "the secret is to push each muscle toward total fiber contraction. When a muscle reaches total contraction, each fiber in the muscle is forced to contract. This increases the size and strength of the fibers, creating bigger and more impressive muscles."[3] The writer goes on to state that locking out too long allows the muscles to rest, and short-circuits your productivity. Many err in their training by spending too much time in the "locked" position. This defeats the purpose of the exercise, which is to maximally stress the muscle. A long lockout takes the stress off for a period of time, and is counter-productive. If you do lock out, it should be very brief. The author of the article on the non-locking out concept goes on to point out that some exercises are better for locking out, and others are better for not locking out. He writes "a simple rule to follow is to never lock out when locking out is easy. If an exercise, like leg extensions, offers optimum contraction at the lockout position, then push to lock it out".[4] Some exercises, particularly those for the biceps, are better performed in a lockout style since more growth comes from the deliberate contraction (as outlined by Aaron Baker in the chapter on biceps). And for the triceps it is often better to use a lockout move on heavier compound lifts such as the triceps bench press, and the weighted dip, and to not lockout on the isolation movements such as the prone press. And you can occasionally perform all types with both the lockout, and the non-lockout approach. The theory behind the non-lockout style is that "the no-lock routine increases resistance, and the more resistance a muscle encounters, the stronger and larger it has to become."[5]

A good visual example of this style of training is seen in the bodybuilding documentary movie *Pumping Iron*, especially during the sessions where **Lou Ferrigno** is seen lifting. Lou often used the non-lock style during the sessions in *Pumping Iron.*

Employ the non-lock style as you train your triceps for some of your exercises. The triceps are primarily a muscle group that use a lot of isolated training techniques, and these lend themselves well to the non-lock repetition. However, remember that many champions also build massive triceps with strong lockout moves. Use both styles.

Triceps Prone Press Variations

There are several effective variations of the triceps prone press. One is to use dumbells instead of the barbell. The dumbell prone press allows for a deeper stretch in the low end of the move and some angling and twisting of the weight to vary the emphasis of the movement. You perform the movement in virtually the same manner as the prone press, but you can bring the dumbell down by the side of the head for the deeper stretch. You can also twist the wrist out on the upward motion to activate the triceps from a different angle.

The reverse grip triceps prone press is performed exactly like the triceps prone press except that you have the palms facing the forehead. This only leaves the thumb to hold the bar so a lighter weight is necessary to prevent the bar from slipping out of your grip. The reverse grip is effective because it changes the stress of the exercise

upon the triceps, and variation is often necessary for continual gains.

The triceps prone press can also be performed with an oval shaped bar with two handles in the centre. This also slightly changes the stress point of the exercise. Still another variation is to use a cable pulley to perform the triceps prone press by placing a bench next to a cable pulley machine.

The triceps prone press or variation can be performed on an incline or decline bench to add further gravity related stress and to keep the muscle under constant tension.

Standing Triceps Press

The standing triceps press is sometimes also called the French Press. The standing triceps press is performed by lowering the barbell behind the head using a narrow grip, then pressing it overhead, utilizing the power of the triceps. The standing triceps press is a good

Lee Priest

Lee Priest uses a rope attachment to perform triceps cable pressdowns.

Finish

Start

these machines are excellent. The Nautilus Triceps Extension machine is one of the more popular and it is used by Mr. Olympia **Dorian Yates**. This machine utilizes the power of the triceps in a single linear approach – you just get in and push as hard as possible. If you use this machine make certain that you use other exercises to totally develop the triceps from all angles since this is a one-angle attack.

Cable Pressdown

If there is one exercise that is used most often by body-builders to work on their triceps, it is the cable pressdown (also called a pushdown). The cable pressdown really pumps up the

mass builder. Don't "cheat" the weight up with an assist from the legs; the more strict the motion the better the results.

Triceps Extension Machine

There are several different machines built specifically for building the triceps. Most of triceps and focuses the action right on the muscles. The cable keeps the tension constant. There is a danger of getting too much rest at the lockout position (arms fully extended downward) so make your lockout extremely brief and contract the triceps head as hard as possible in the lockout position. Rotate between brief lockouts and no lockouts every couple of repetitions. Strict form is crucial for the best results in the triceps cable pressdown.

For real results, perform all cable pressdown extension work in very strict form.

Sonny Schmidt

You can vary the effect of the pressdown by using different bar attachments (straight, angled, rope, etc). Try a couple to find the one that works best for your body.

A variation of the triceps cable pressdown is the one-arm version. This exercise is performed with a single cable pulley handle and allows you to concentrate on one triceps at a time. You can get a tremendous pump using the one-arm triceps cable pressdown. You can also reverse the grip and produce slightly different stresses on the muscle. Use the triceps cable pressdown often for maximal pumps.

One-Arm Dumbell Extension

The one-arm dumbell extension is a great exercise for filling out the full length of the triceps muscle group – provided you perform it correctly. The correct manner to perform the one-arm dumbell extension is to raise a dumbell overhead, and lift the upper arm straight up in the air. Keep the arm straight up throughout the exercise, moving only the lower arm.

For the one-arm dumbell extension to be effective, keep the upper arm straight up and immobile during the exercise, moving the weight with motion only in the lower arm.

Let the upper arm remain as stiff and straight as a flagpole, and concentrate the motion on the lower arm (moving the dumbell from behind the neck to straight up, and back) and pushed by the triceps. That is, the motion of the lower arm comes from the triceps moving it, not from a shoulder movement.

It takes a lot of intense concentration to perform this exercise correctly, but it is worth the effort for a triceps with full-length development looks terrific.

Triceps Dumbell Kickback

The triceps dumbell kickback is a movement that must be performed in the right manner to get the right effect. The body is bent over almost parallel to the floor, while grasping a dumbell in one hand and supporting your frame

with the other. Keep the elbow in your side fairly tight, and "kick" the dumbell back to full extension of the triceps, a point where the upper arm is about parallel with the floor. As you kick the dumbell back and up, do so slowly to let the triceps perform the action. There is a tendency to let momentum build after a couple of repetitions so that the last several reps are performed via momentum instead of through triceps power. Resist this mistake and slow your motion down a couple of levels. Experiment with the angles on this movement.

Triceps Pushup

The triceps pushup is to the triceps muscle what the close-grip chinup is to the biceps – an excellent free-hand exercise. The triceps pushup is performed by doing a basic

Shawn Ray and Lee Haney

pushup, except that the hands are placed much closer together (about six inches apart). This close placement of the hands shifts the primary emphasis of the move from the chest to the triceps. As with all free-hand exercises, the triceps pushup has limitations because its primary stimulation comes through bodyweight. To make the movement more challenging, perform it with the feet on a higher level. This exercise is good for when you do not have access to weights yet need to hit the triceps hard.

The triceps pushup is also a good move for getting a final pump into the arms at the end of a workout.

Kneeling Triceps Cable Extension

The kneeling triceps cable extension is performed with a cable pulley system. Grasp the high cable, and kneel forward. If possible, support your elbows on a bench. Press the cable forward as far as possible, then slowly let the cable move back until your triceps are fully stretched. This movement is a combination of the triceps extension and the cable pushdown. It works the full range of the triceps.

Putting it Together

These are some of the many triceps exercises available for building your arms. This grouping represents the best

Mike Ashley

of those exercises. Training the triceps is a fairly basic, straightforward groove that you get your arms into. The different exercises are important, but more important is how you use them.

Unless your triceps are already gigantic, you will need to focus on putting some size into them. This translates into performing at least one muscle mass builder per triceps workout.

Without specifically aiming at building bigger triceps, your triceps will obtain some shape but remain unimpressive. Triceps size is essential for animal arms.

For building triceps shape it is important to use a variety of different exercises and to perform the exercises in good form. Don't get stuck with only one triceps routine all of the

Eddie Robinson

time. **Remember that the triceps make up about 66 percent of the upper arm size.** If you want animal arms, it is essential to really work your triceps hard and heavy.

Hand Position and Body Angle

The position of your hands and the angle of your body are both very important to maximizing your triceps workout. For instance, if you place your hands wide in the dip or pushup movement, you will focus the action onto the chest muscles instead of the triceps. For both of these movements, the narrow position is one that works the triceps. How narrow? Quite narrow. However, since each bodybuilder is of a different height, and has a different bone structure in the arms and shoulder girdle, it is not good to give any exact measurements (such as a command to place your hands exactly 23 inches apart with absolutely no deviation from that width). You will need to find the positions, angles, and hand placements that work for you. It is wise to pay attention to the stimulation that any of a variety of different hand positions and angles cause to your triceps – write the data down in a notebook. Record the width or angle you used and find, over time, just the right one for you. Some hand positions and angles will hit your triceps right on the head and others won't really do much for them. It is very important to experiment with many different triceps variables in body angle and hand position. Remember, the positions that bring the deepest burning sensation to your triceps are those that are most effective.

You can build bigger and better triceps if you work the weights intensely and wisely, giving the muscles reason to grow, and then the nutrition and rest in which to do so.

There are several top bodybuilders who have developed awesome triceps. The routines and tips from those who have successfully built bigger arms are included in the "Triceps Addendum" that follows at the end of this chapter. Peruse the addendum. There are also some triceps workout combinations that you can experiment with. If you find some that work for you then go with those. Or you may want to add something to one of the workouts or remove an exercise that is not working for you. Don't be satisfied with anything less than building the best arms possible. Triceps make a major contribution to animal arms.

1. Arnold Schwarzenegger and Douglas Kent Hall, "Arnold: The Education of a Bodybuilder," (New York: Wallaby Pocket Books, 1977) p. 215
2. Robert Kennedy, "Beef It," New York: Sterling Publishing Company, 1984) p. 124
3. Brett McQuade, "Locking into Muscle Growth," *MuscleMag International*, April 1995, p. 104
4. Ibid, p. 105
5. Ibid

Lee Priest

Triceps Addendum

Hard Core
Triceps bench presses
3 x 6-10 repetitions
Weighted dips
3 x 10-20 repetitions
Triceps prone presses
3 x 10-15 repetitions

Alternate 1
Triceps pressdowns
4 x 6-12 repetitions
One-arm triceps extensions
4 x 6-12 repetitions
Reverse dips
2 x 10-20 repetitions

Alternate 2
Standing French presses
5 x 8-10 repetitions
Close-grip bench presses
5 x 12-15 repetitions
One-arm cable pushdowns
2 x 6-12 repetitions

Heavy Duty
Weighed dips
2 x 6-10 repetitions
Nautilus triceps extensions
2 x 6-10 repetitions

Free Hand Workout
Triceps dips
3-4 x 20-30 repetitions
Close grip push-ups
3-4 x 30-40 repetitions
Reverse dips
2 x 25 repetitions

The Champions' Workouts

Vince Taylor's triceps workout:[1]
One-arm cable reverse pushdowns
5 x 6-12 repetitions
Taylor cable "salutes"
5 x6-12 repetitions
Overhead cable triceps extensions
5 x 6-12 repetitions
Overhead power triceps pushdowns
5 x6-12 repetitions

Craig Titus
Craig Titus' triceps training philosophy centers around basic movements and heavy, heavy weights. Craig used his heavy but basic approach to go from 18.25 inch arms to 20 inch arms in just 16 months. Each set of his workouts are taken to complete muscular failure. Craig rests more between the power triceps exercises (2 to 3 minutes on most sets; 2 to 5 on maximum attempts). He occasionally performs the rear triceps dip. Craig often does the same exercises but changes the sequence.[2]

Craig Titus

Craig Titus' triceps workout:[3]

Close-grip bench presses
5 x 3-15 repetitions
Lying prone presses
4 x 9-12 repetitions
One-arm dumbell extensions
4 x 9-12 repetitions
Triceps cable pushdowns
4 x 20 repetitions

Mr. Olympia Dorian Yates triceps workout:[4]

Nautilus triceps extensions
2 warm-up sets, 1 hot 6-8 repetitions
Pressdowns
1 x 6-8 repetitions

Master's Mr. Olympia

Big Sonny Schmidt has massive triceps, and they helped him take the Master's title.

Sonny Schmidt's triceps workout:[5]

Lying triceps extensions
5 x 10-15 repetitions
Pressdowns
5 x 10-15 repetitions
One-arm cable pressdowns
5 x 10-15 repetitions

Robby Robinson's triceps workout:

Two-arm pushdowns
4 x8-10 repetitions
One-arm dumbell triceps extensions
4 x 8-10 repetitions
One-arm cable pressdowns
4 x 8-10 repetitions

Rick Valente's triceps workout:[6]

Pressdowns
3-5 x 6-8 repetitions, 1 set of 35 repetitions
Lying triceps extensions
3-5 x 6-8 repetitions, 1 set of 35 repetitions
Standing triceps extensions
3-5 x 6-8 repetitions, 1 set of 35 repetitions

Sergio Oliva

One of the largest (perhaps the largest) pair of triceps belong to the massive Sergio Oliva. If you want to build some animal triceps, it would be wise to take a look at Sergio's triceps workout, recorded by Norman Zale in the January 1994 edition of *MuscleMag International*.

Sergio Oliva's triceps workout:

For his triceps Sergio is very fond of doing a number of different exercises using a single pulley. After doing five or six sets of standing triceps extensions, using progressively heavier weights with each set, he will begin a nonstop series of five pulley exercises that last approximately 25 minutes. These are done one arm at a time, and he alternates arms until all five sets of one exercise are completed and then immediately begins the next exercise. The five pulley exercises that he favors are:

1. One arm triceps curls behind neck, is similar to the same exercise that is done with a dumbell. With one arm extended overhead, he bends his arm until the forearm rests along his upper arm and then immediately straightens his arm overhead. This exercise is done on a low pulley attachment.

The next three movements are performed on a pulley arrangement that is approximately five feet off the floor.

Eddie Robinson

Andreas Munzer

2. Horizontal triceps extensions to the side are performed while standing with his left arm straight and his hand braced against the frame for support. The pulley handle is held in his right hand and he proceeds to bend the right arm until his hand almost touches his neck and then extends the arm directly to the side as he attempts to maintain his elbow above the horizontal plane. As with other exercises he alternates arms.

3. Triceps extensions to the front are very similar to the above exercise. With his back to the pulley, and one arm extended to the front while the elbow is supported with the opposite hand, Sergio bends and straightens the working arm directly in front of him.

4. Next he does triceps pushdowns, which are the same as lat machine pushdowns but he uses only one arm at a time. One occasion he will reverse his hand position so that the palm is facing up rather than down.

5. To finish off this series of exercises, Sergio returns to the lower pulley. Facing the pulley and bending forward from the waist, he does kickbacks while bracing the working arm against his side. Keeping it in this position, he bends his arm, straightens it to the rear, and further raises his arm five or six inches beyond the horizontal position in order to get a deep muscle ache and cramp his triceps to the utmost. **Twenty-five sets of strict triceps work leaves Sergio's arms looking like legs!** On his arm days he again does many sets of dips, usually 20 to 25 reps per set without any additional weight, and these are spread out throughout the workout.[7]

Ronnie Coleman

Another bodybuilder with awesome triceps is big **Ronnie Coleman**. Ronnie is 5'11" tall, weighs 230 pounds and has arms that are over 21 inches. His massive triceps make up much of that measurement. How does he train them? Brian Dobson revealed how in *MuscleMag International*:

For triceps Ronnie has recently been experimenting with pulley movements and finding that they provide a great stretch and contraction with constant tension on the muscle. They are also easier on the elbow joints than many traditional triceps exercises like skull-crushers and French presses. Pushdowns are a great all-around triceps exercise. They also get the elbows warmed up for the following movements. Ronnie does a warmup of 25 to 30 reps with 80 pounds. He will then follow with three progressively heavier sets of up to 200 pounds or more to failure (generally 10 to 15 reps). A final lighter set of 20 to 30 strict, contracted reps with 100 pounds really brings out the striations.

Overhead cable extensions with a rope work the long inner triceps heads to make the arms larger and fuller appearing. Ronnie always gets a good stretch and makes sure to contract at the extension to bring out the striations. After a warmup Ronnie does 3 x 15 to 25 reps.

To work the inside head of the triceps he will use single-arm overhead dumbell extensions or the two-arm dumbell extension. These can be touchy on the elbow joints so make sure your elbows are warm before trying. Ronnie does a warmup of 20 to 25 reps with 35 pounds, then jumps up to 60 plus pounds for 3 x 10 to 12 reps. The final exercise is the two-arm dumbell kickback. This is an extremely effective exercise when done in strict form, holding the dumbell in the finished or kick-backed position for 1-2 seconds. A heavy weight is not necessary. Ronnie performs 3-4 sets of 10-15 reps with 30-35 pounds.[8]

Here is a summary of Ronnie's triceps routine:

1. Pushdowns
1 warmup x 25-35 reps
3 x 10-15 reps to failure
1 x 20-30 reps

2. Overhead cable extensions
1 warmup x 15 reps
2 x 15-25 reps to failure

3. Single- or two-arm overhead dumbell extensions
1 warmup x 20-25 reps
3 x 10-12 reps to failure

4. Two-arm dumbell kickbacks
3-4 x 10-15 reps to failure

Aaron Baker

Aaron Baker is a champion body-builder who has massive arms, and he has worked to make his triceps incredible enough to match his awesome biceps. Aaron has arms that are beautifully bal-anced, with both the biceps and triceps containing sweeping massive curves of muscle. T.C. Luoma wrote in *MuscleMag International* on Aaron's arm training. For his triceps, Aaron says "I've always preferred the first exercise in a workout to be the mass builder, so I start my triceps training with lying triceps exten-sions with an EZ-curl bar. I lower the bar over the top of my head until my fore-arms are slightly below parallel with the floor. I keep my elbows pointed at the ceiling, very close to my body, so we're talking about a pretty deep stretch here. I lock out at the top, but not over my chin or chest. I lock out more over the bridge of my nose. That way the tension stays on the triceps."[9] Aaron likes to stay in the same general set and rep range (four sets of 8 to 12 reps) that he uses for biceps training.

After extensions, Aaron moves on to cable pushdowns. "I prefer to use a short bar with a slight downward angle to it. I keep a close grip, with my upper body slightly bent, elbows tight, and I let the bar come up to my chin. I push down slowly, and I lock out at the bottom. Isola-tion is very important here. I try not to throw the body in and out of the movement. If I'm training triceps, it's a party for triceps only, so I don't want to be hanging over the cable and throwing my shoulders and back into the movement."[10]

Aaron's third triceps movement is seat-ed dumbell extensions over the head. "I do these using one dumbell at a time, and I try to keep my head erect instead of tipping it. I almost always do it in front of a mirror. I square off my hips and shoulders and look straight ahead. With the elbow pointed up at the ceiling, I extend the arm."[11] Although many people use the free arm to support the working arm, Aaron prefers to keep his other arm out of the way so he can get the desired isolation. His other arm is usually holding onto the bench or grabbing his "bat-belt."

The last exercise in Aaron's arm attack is triceps kickback. "I like to get on a flat bench

Check out the triceps.
– Aaron Baker and
Flex Wheeler

– with the knee opposite to the triceps I'm working on the bench, and the other leg extended out behind me. I align the upper arm with the floor, so that when the weight is fully extended, it's parallel to the floor too. I also try to pause at the top of the movement. I acknowledge the contraction, and try to slowly control the negative on the way down. It's always a fluid movement, and it's slow and controlled...I think the more basic an exercise is, the better. You can get fancy, you can paint it, but you still have to make sure it works. You can do all the shaping movements in the world, but if you're not building muscle, then you're painting it before you get it running."[12]

Dave Fisher

Dave Fisher is similar to Aaron in that he also has big triceps and believes in the basics. He says "I must say that I'm not a big believer in this exercise hitting the inside of the triceps or that exercise hitting the outer part of the triceps. Every triceps exercise you do hits the whole muscle. Sometimes one exercise may stress a little more of one part than the other, but it's not really that significant. Sticking to the basics and going heavy is what's going to

make you get bigger triceps. You could get huge triceps just doing one exercise, and who's to say that, once it got all shredded, it wouldn't look just as good as someone's who did all the different exercises to get the same size...Here's what I like to do: I use pushdowns, lying extensions, cable extension, one-arm overhead extensions, and what they call French presses (seated overhead barbell extensions). These are the exercises that I can use a lot of weight on and therefore should give me the mass increases I'm looking for. I only pick two exercises per workout, and do only two (three at the most) all-out working sets with max weight and to total failure. This doesn't include warmups, of course, and that could be three or four sets, depending upon how cold I am or how I'm feeling that day. I don't go for the all-out set until I'm sure that the muscle is fully ready to handle the extreme punishment it's about to get. The last thing I want to do is get injured. My choice of two exercises each workout is in no way scientific, just what I feel like doing that day. I use different exercises mostly to keep from getting bored – and just in case all those theories about different exercises for different bodyparts of the muscle

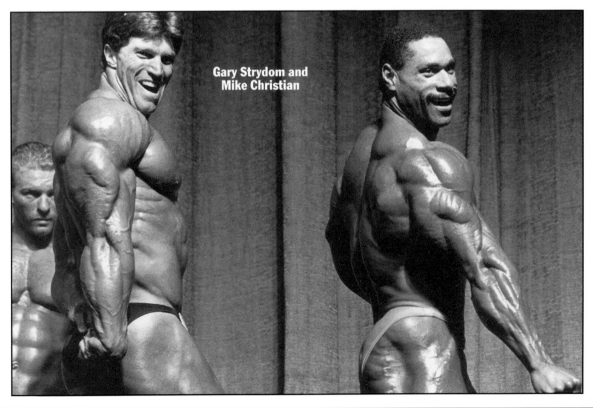

Gary Strydom and
Mike Christian

Shawn Ray

Single-arm triceps extensions in a pushdown motion
6 sets
Single-arm triceps extensions with a twist motion
6 sets

Jason Marcovici's triceps workout:[15]
Workout 1
Lying EZ-bar triceps extensions
4 x 8-12 (pyramiding up in weight each set)
Triceps pushdowns
3-4 x 6-8 (pyramiding up in weight each set)
One-arm cable kickbacks
3-4 x 12-15
or
Triceps dips between benches
(with plates on his lap)

Workout 2
Kneeling rope extensions
4-7 x 6-10
One-arm kickbacks
4 x 10-12
Weighted triceps dips
4 x 12-15 or
Overhead rope extensions
4 x 10-12

THREE - ADDENDUM

are true, why take any chances, eh? I train my triceps once a week on back day, sometimes before back, and sometimes after. That's it."[13]

Mohamed Makkawy's triceps workout:
Mohamed Makkawy is another bodybuilder with superb triceps. One of his triceps routines included:
Lying triceps extensions
Two-dumbell triceps kickbacks
Kneeling rope-pulley extensions
Machine triceps extensions
He performed these exercises for three circuits.[14]

Flex Wheeler's triceps workout:
Triceps pushdowns with V-handle
6 sets

1. Reg Bradford, "Huge, Massive, Freaky Arm Routine," *Muscular Development*, February 1996, pp. 59-63
2. Greg Zulak, "Craig Titus's Titan Workouts for Terrific Triceps," *MuscleMag International*, April 1995, pp. 168-169
3. Ibid
4. Bill Geiger and Dorian Yates, "How I won the Mr. Olympia," *Muscle & Fitness*, January 1996, p. 76
5. Marty Gallagher, "How he won the Masters Olympia," *Muscle & Fitness*, January 1996, p. 86
6. Marty Gallagher, "Arms by Valente," *Muscle & Fitness*, August 1995, p. 187
7. Norman Zale, "Sergio," *MuscleMag International*, January1994, pp. 34-35
8. Brian Dobson, "Ronnie Coleman's Arms," *MuscleMag International*, January 1994, pp. 20-22
9. T.C. Luoma, "Armed Warfare," *MuscleMag International*, May/June 1991, pp. 118-120
10. Ibid
11. Ibid
12. Ibid
13. Dave Fisher, "Body by Fisher," *MuscleMag International*, Jan 1995, p. 220
14. Chris Lund, "Makkawy's Arms," *MuscleMag International*, June 1983, p. 35, 74
15. Greg Zulak, "Massive Marcovici," *MuscleMag International,* August 1994, p. 66

Ronnie Coleman

The forearms are one of the most overlooked muscle groups in bodybuilding. Often you find routines that work every other muscle group but skip working the forearms. And there is some reason for that – some bodybuilders have fantastic forearms purely from genetics – they were born with the disposition to have good forearm development regardless of how they trained that section of the arm. But this is not true of everyone. And even some who have been blessed with better forearm genetics still train the forearms very hard anyway. These would include **Casey Viator** and **Lee Haney**, both of whom have massive muscular forearm development.

Casey Viator

Chapter Four

The Forearms: Pillars of Power

Another factor is that of the secondary effect of training other body parts. When you lift weights for almost all upper-body movements, and some lower-body movements, you use the forearm muscles to control the bar(s). Even with a leg movement like the squat there is some forearm involvement. The leg extension is similar – you brace your body with a hand hold, and that comes through the forearms. The forearms are involved in so many different exercises that they get a lot of work. And for some bodybuilders, this provides enough stimulation for good development. But for many others, it does not, and there is need for further stimulation of the forearm muscles. This further stimulation comes through direct and specific training for that area of the arm, the forearm. The focus of this chapter is on the development of the forearm.

Crucial Link

The forearms are the link between that which picks up and holds the weight (the hands) and the muscles that are being used to lift the weight (shoulders, biceps, etc.). It is very important that the forearm be powerful in order to allow for use of the heavier iron needed to add muscle mass. If your hands and forearms can't handle heavy iron, then you cannot use the weight to train other body parts. The forearms can be a weak link if they are not correctly developed. Weak forearms can cause a lifter to fail in movements like the deadlift and heavy dumbell presses. If this occurs, the only thing holding the lifter back is lack of forearm work. The other bigger body parts are strong enough to handle the weight but do not get the oppor-

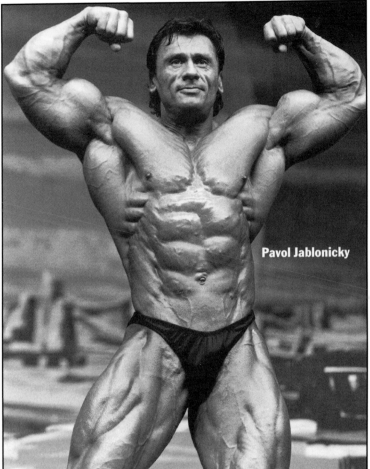

Pavol Jablonicky

see most people you are attired in something that covers most of you up except for your neck and forearms.

Integrated arms

Another consideration for working on the forearms is that even if the biceps and triceps were not covered up, the whole arm would look weird if the forearms were underdeveloped. For an arm to look great there has to be a balance between the biceps, triceps, and also the forearm. The muscular development of the arms must be integrated to make the muscles "flow." If any of the three major muscle groups are out of sync, they all look bad. If someone has massive biceps and tiny triceps, you notice that right away. And that is also true of the tie-in between the upper and lower arms. If either is out of balance with the other the entire appearance is skewed. Imagine a pair of 20 inch upper arms with 9 inch forearms, or 17 inch forearms and 14 inch upper arms. For the arms to look totally fantastic you have to put some time in on forearm work unless you are one of the genetically gifted few who have awesome forearms from the beginning.

Forged Forearms

Men of the past had great forearms because of more manual labor. Their forearms were forged through hard work. It was tough work digging a living out of the ground, or in the field. Milking a cow was one way that large forearms were developed by many men in the past. The forearms have bore the brunt of a lot of labor throughout history. The simple but tough struggle to survive included a lot of work that required strong forearms. Recently, in the past few decades, with the mechanization and computerization of most everything the forearms are not used as much. They are usually smaller in comparison with the forearms of our forefathers. However, that can be remedied through weight training. You do not have to despair if

tunity to grow because of the failure of the forearms. And if this happens on a regular basis, the larger body parts will atrophy.

If this is not enough to convince you to put in some dedicated and consistent effort on the forearms, there is more. Which muscle is seen the most by everyone? It is a toss-up between the forearms and the neck. And certainly the part of the arm most visible to the world is the forearm. The biceps and triceps are often covered up by shirts, suits, and coats. However, the forearm is often visible. If someone sees a mediocre or poor forearm, then the natural assumption is that the rest of the arm and body is also second rate. And you may never have an opportunity to change that opinion! You don't take your shirt off all that much in civilized society so you might not get that chance to show off your big upper arm to just anyone. It is a rarity when the body is displayed outside of the posing platform or the beach, and when you your forearms are sub-par, but you will have to put some work in on transforming them into a more massively muscled bodypart.

Frequency

Training the biceps and triceps should be rather infrequent – you should give each muscle group some significant rest between workouts, especially if you are in a heavy-duty intense mode (for instance, **Michael Francois** takes up to 10 days between biceps workouts).[1] And Mr. Olympia, **Dorian Yates**, preaches the importance of sufficient rest. However, this approach of a lot of rest between workouts does not necessarily hold true for the forearms. You can train the forearms more frequently, up to once a day or more, since the muscle tissue in the forearm is of a density and type that recuperates quickly and takes quite a bit of work without much damage. The advertising line of the Timex watch applies to the forearm – "it takes a licking and keeps on ticking." The forearms are tough and can handle more frequent workouts. Don't be afraid to push them to the limit several times a week. Experiment and find what routine rotation is best for your forearms.

Sets and Reps

There is some debate on how many sets and repetitions are necessary for building up the forearms muscles. Some argue that the forearms should be trained with the same approach to sets and repetitions (medium range) as the rest of the muscle groups. Fitness writer Jerry Robinson states that the best repetition ranges for forearm work fall in the 6 to 8 and 8 to 10 repetition groups.[2] However, many others point out that the forearms can handle a higher load, and need more repetitions, and sometimes more sets. However, since the forearms get secondary work with many of the other exercises, the set range can be low to moderate (1 to 3 sets per exercise) and 1 to 3 direct forearm exercises can be used. The repetitions should be fairly high to create a real burn in the forearms for full growth in size and strength. An occasional shock workout is also in order. Fitness writer Greg Merritt points out that you should "occasionally do mega-reps. Once a month or so grab a very light weight and pound out a few sets of 100 repetitions in one or more exercises. This con-

centration will get your lower arms burning and shock them into new growth."[3]

Iron for forearms

As with the other muscle groups of the arms, the best way to train the forearms is through incrementally tougher challenges. And this is best done with weights. However, with the forearms, there are many other manners to increase the muscularity, and these will be discussed in this chapter.

The Exercises

Many exercises involve the use of the forearms but some are better than others. Don't be shy in adding an exercise that you find works

Mike Matarazzo

particularly well for your forearms. You may discover some different exercise or movement that really hits the forearms hard – use it.

The Deadlift

Although many people view the deadlift as a pure powerlifting movement, it has many beneficial factors for the bodybuilder. In addition to building up the back and jazzing the overall metabolism of all muscles, the deadlift also places a very high emphasis on the forearm. The tremendous poundages used in the deadlift are held by the grip of the hands, which are moved and set firmly in place by the forearms. By lifting a lot of weight in the deadlift you also build up your forearms.

There is a manner by which the deadlift can be particularly effective. That is with an overgrip. Most people who use deadlift use a "mixed" grip, with one hand in an overgrip position (fingers facing down) and the other hand in an undergrip position like that used for a curl. This "mixed" grip is great for ensuring that you are able to lift the weight better but it is not the ultimate for building the forearms. A better way to build the forearms is with both hands in the overgrip position.

To get maximum benefits, take your overgrip deadlift as heavy as you can for 3-8 repetitions. Push it to the point where the weight is so heavy that it starts to slip through your hands. Stay at that weight for a while, then add 2.5 to 5 pounds (you can obtain a pair of 1.25 weights at some outlets). By only increasing your deadlift poundage by these small amounts your forearms and hands gradually get used to the heavy weight and the new strength allows you to move up to a heavier deadlift. This will build bigger and stronger forearms. Since the deadlift involves some of the most heavy weight you will be moving it serves to really ignite forearm growth. Include some deadlift work in your arm routine (although the deadlifting does not necessarily have to be on the same day that you do biceps or triceps). When you deadlift you do not need to concentrate on the forearms (provided you are using an overgrip for

both hands), the lift will do the trick, and the growth in size and strength will occur in response.

The Wrist Curl

Another effective and very popular exercise for the forearm is the wrist curl. It puts direct action onto the forearm. The wrist curl is performed by placing the wrists close together, supporting them on a bench (seated, by the edge) and lowering the weight by dropping the hands in a downward extension. At the bottom, where the hands can extend no further without dropping the weight, the motion is reversed, and the weight is brought back up on the strength of the forearm muscles. It is important to let the hands sit in the far downward position for a second to stop any motion so that the full action

Rich Gaspari demonstrates the wrist curl.
– *Start*

of the lift is one of muscle action, not weight momentum. When you use momentum in any lift you take away from its effectiveness. This is especially crucial in movements where the range of motion is rather short, and such is the case with the wrist curl. Go slow.

The wrist curl can also be performed in a reverse manner, with the hands extending upward off the bench. Use both the regular and reverse grips for training with the wrist curl.

The Hand Grip

A practical way to train the forearms is with the hand grip. This little A-shaped exercise item is sold in most sporting goods stores. It often comes in a variety of different strength ranges, and the tension varies from low to very tough. Some mail-order companies sell elite hand grip units. The hand gripper is great for getting in a stimulating workout on the forearms when you don't have an opportunity to use the weights. Since the difficulty of the unit generally cannot be increased except by an increase in repetitions (there are some units that do allow for progressive increases and are sold in many bodybuilding magazines) they provide a limited development range. However, since the forearm muscles are geared more toward a high repetition response, the hand gripper will give your forearms a good growth spurt and are a good exercise to use on a frequent basis.

Off-Set Lift

The off-set lift is fantastic for isolating the forearm muscles. This exercise is performed with an off-set weight – you load one end of a dumbell with weights and leave the other end empty (of course you will have to place collars on the weights). Extend your arm with the off-set dumbell in hand, and lower the weighted end of the dumbell by placing your wrist in a downward motion. Raise the weight by raising your wrist. Repeat until you fail to be able to lift the weight, then switch and do the same for the other arm. Make certain that your forearm remains rigid and parallel to the floor to avoid cheating (which can occur if you assist the motion with a little biceps sway). You can also work this to the rear by placing the weighted end of the dumbell behind you, and making a similar motion as with the frontal movement. Since this exercise utilizes weights, you can really in-crease the poundage over a period of time and build up some awesome forearm muscularity.

Finish

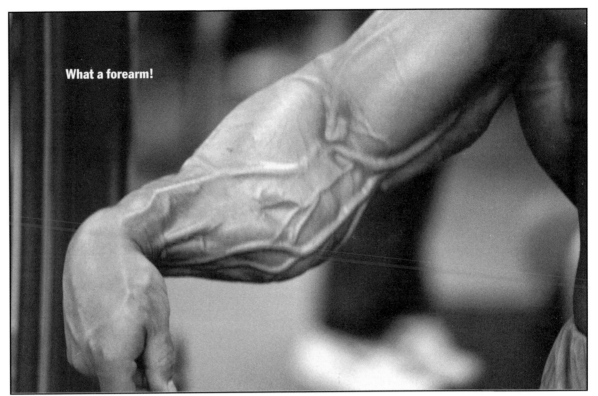

What a forearm!

Brachialis bi-product

The exercises that build up the brachialis muscle are also very effective on the forearms. This includes the hammer curl, the zottman curl, and the reverse curl. Any one of these exercises, performed on a regular basis, will develop some very noticeable size and strength in the forearms in addition to the brachialis. One brachialis/forearm movement per arm workout should be sufficient provided you put in an all-out intense effort for the sets and repetitions that you choose to do.

Super Tip – Use the brachialis/forearm exercises often. They work several parts of the arm and give very noticeable results in a short period of time.

Wrist Roll-ups

An exercise that is excruciatingly tough but just as effective as it is painful is the weighted wrist roll-up. This is performed by rolling up a weight that is attached to a handle structure by a cord. You hold the handle out with your forearms fairly rigid and parallel to the floor. Roll the weight up by moving the handle forward or backward until the cord is wound all the way up and the weight touches the handle, then slowly reverse the process until the weight is again on the floor. This exercise will really burn in the forearms – take it as far as you can into the pain barrier for effective results. After performing a set, reverse the motion to stimulate the muscles from the opposite direction.

You can buy a wrist roller through the advertising pages of a bodybuilding or fitness magazine. Some sporting goods carry them. And you can make your own. Simply purchase a stout cord, 2-4 inch steel ring, and a piece of 2 inch PVC pipe that is about a foot and a half in length. Drill a hole through the pipe, and attach the cord to it. Then attach the cord to the steel ring in a manner that can be quickly detached (an eyelet clip works well). Add weight to the cord by putting on plates attached to the steel ring end of the device. Add or detach weight as necessary until you find the right amount to stimulate your forearms. This exercise really builds some solid forearm muscle.

Putty Power

There have been several advances in the training of the forearms thorough various exercise measures. One of these is through putty. Several years ago the fad was a child's toy titled "Silly Putty," a putty that could be formed into various shapes, and then returned to a ball of the putty. Physical therapists have recently been using a similar type of substance to re-train the hand movements of people who have been injured. Different companies have developed putty at different strength levels. This stuff is great for building the forearms, because when the hands are trained at an intense level, so are the forearms. Various forms of this substance are now on the market, and can be used to work on your hands and forearms throughout the day.

Balls of Fire

Sporting balls can also be used to develop powerful forearms. The best are racquet balls. These can be squeezed in a high repetition manner and the forearms receive a great workout. A tougher test is the tennis ball, which calls for more hand and forearm strength to master. A good approach is to start with racquetball and work with it until you have mastered it, then move up to a tennis ball. There are a variety of other hand-sized balls that you can use to build up your forearm strength so buy a couple (they are usually very cheap) and experiment.

Milos Sarcev

Bands

A stout rubber band can also build up the forearm. Place the band on the end of your fingertips (bring all of the fingers together into a point), then expand your fingers outward. Repeat for high repetitions. This type of training serves a dual purpose. In addition to building your forearms, this exercise also is helpful in reducing the problem of "tennis elbow" that many bodybuilders develop from the stress on their elbows during certain movements (such as triceps work). Get a strong, thick, tight rubber band and work on your forearm strength, and also receive the benefit of reducing elbow problems. Rubber band training is essentially free – you can get a rubber band most anywhere.

Behind-the-Back Wrist Curls

Another unique and unusual form of the wrist curl is the behind-the-back wrist curl. This exercise is performed by holding a barbell behind your back. From this point you use your hands only to curl the weight up, then lower again.

Forearm Priority

Make forearm training a main part of your arm program instead of a sideline, especially if you need some improvement in this

Michael Francois

Workout 6
Power putty, 10 minutes of gripping
Reverse curls, 3 x 12 repetitions

Forearm Tips and Workouts from the Champions
**Seven-time Mr. Olympia,
Arnold Schwarzenegger's forearm training program:**
5 x 10-15 repetitions of the wrist curl.[4]
**Master's Olympia Champion
Sonny Schmidt's forearm training program:**
Wrist curls, 5 x 15-20 repetitions[5]

Dorian Yates

area. Aim your training at the goal of balanced arms, with forearms that can fit in with your biceps and triceps. Get in a few intense sets of direct forearm training at least once a week.

Forearm Workouts
Workout 1
Wrist curls, 3 x 8-10 repetitions
Hammer curls, 2 x 12 repetitions

Workout 2
Wrist roll-ups, 2 sets
Hand grip exercises, 3 sets of as many repetitions as possible

Workout 3
Overgrip deadlifts, 3 x 5-8 repetitions, heavy weight
Reverse wrist curls, 2 x 12-15 repetitions

Workout 4
Heavy wrist curls, 2 x 6-8 repetitions
Heavy reverse curls, 2 sets of 6-8 repetitions

Workout 5
Light wrist curls, 2 x 50 repetitions
Hand grips, 5 sets of as many repetitions as possible

Milos Sarcev's forearm training program:
EZ-bar reverse curls
Hammer curls
Wrist curls off a bench
Wrist curls, standing and behind the back

     Mishko will pick some of these exercises and perform several sets of each. One example would be 4 sets of hammer curls and four sets of wrist curls.[6]

     Another top bodybuilder who thought wrist curls were beneficial was **Steve Reeves**, who said "forearm wrist curls are good for those who need work in this area."[7] Steve had forearms that measured almost 15 inches.

Lee Haney
108

Ronnie Coleman

Lee Labrada's comments on forearm training:

     "I am fortunate in that I never have to work my forearms directly. I get enough forearm stimulation from my regular back and biceps exercises by gripping the bar hard. I never do wrist curls, but I will do hammer curls to work the area below the biceps-elbow area."[8]

     Ronnie Coleman does hammer curls to develop his forearms.[9] They have served him well.

     If you notice, the two exercises that the champions use the most for building their forearms are the wrist curl, and the hammer curl. If you want animal forearms, use these specific exercises to get there.

1. Mike Francois, "Ungodly Guns," *Flex*, January 1996, p. 62
2. Jerry Robinson, "Power Forearms," *Muscle & Fitness*, October 1994, p. 124
3. Greg Merritt, "Don't forget the forearms," *MuscleMag International*, April 1995, p. 100.
4. Arnold Schwarzenegger & Douglas Kent Hall, "Arnold: The Education of a Bodybuilder," (New York: Wallaby Books, 1977), p. 238
5. Marty Gallagher, "How He Won the Masters Olympia," *Muscle & Fitness*, January 1996, p. 86
6. Greg Zulak, "The way to Balanced Arms," *MuscleMag International*, June 1993, pp. 24 & 26
7. John Little, "Steve Reeves, The man, The legend," MuscleMag International, July 1991, p. 78
8. Greg Zulak, "Lee Labrada's biceps," *MuscleMag International*, May/ June 1991, p. 140
9. Brian Dobson, "Ronnie Coleman's Arms," *MuscleMag International*, January 1994, p. 20

ANIMAL FOUR ARMS

Sue Gafner and Milos Sarcev

There are several tips on training the arms and training the physique in general that can provide very valuable assistance in building awesome arms. In this chapter a variety of those tips will be given for additional ideas and incentive that will fuel your fire for animal arms.

Chapter Five

Awesome Arm Training Tips

away, then lower the body back again. Repeat for several repetitions until the triceps are pumped up to an extremely massive size.

Power Pose:
After a biceps workout, pose in front of a mirror and flex your biceps as hard as possible, powerfully contracting them. Flex the biceps and put the hand of the non-flexed arm against the wrist of the flexed arm. Pull the wrist of the flexed arm against the non-flexed arm for resistance and watch as the biceps reaches up for a higher peak.

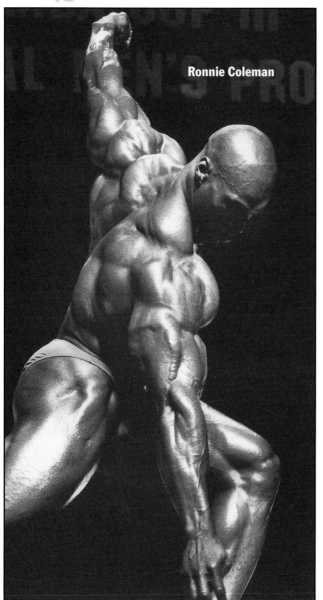

Ronnie Coleman

Mike Ashley

Super Tips

Power Pump:
At the end of a triceps workout, pump out several "bent" pushups by leaning over at a 45 degree angle and grasping the bar on a bench with a narrow grip and push your body out and

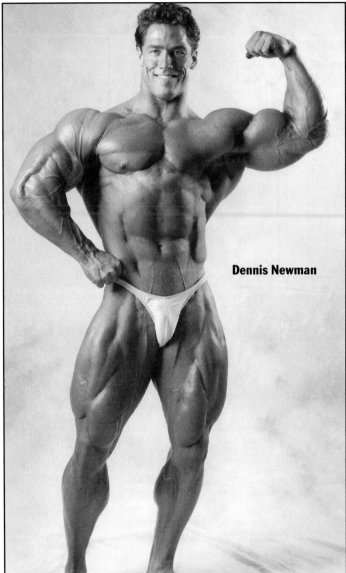

Dennis Newman

up to large overall increases. If you still need more arm size, continue to focus on triceps mass and biceps height until you get the growth you want.

Water:
Take plenty of water before, during, and after your arm training workouts. Don't fall into a state of semi-dehydration.

Champions Training Tips

Don Long's outlook:
"I'm never gonna let anything bring me down. I'm not gonna be lazy. I'm gonna be a Dorian Yates. He never lets anything slow him down. He's a monster. He's always training."[1]

Don Long's training approach:
"When I started training I had a lean, symmetrical body. I needed size. I wanted mass – everywhere. I knew that if I attacked every bodypart with equal intensity I would grow – but I would grow balanced!"[2]

Don Long's biceps training advice:
"I had a good mind to muscle connection with my arms. I always felt my biceps working during the exercise. A person can learn to feel the biceps while training, but if you naturally have a good feel when you start training you'll be ahead of the game. In the past, I did four biceps exercises, but realized I could cut back. I train hard. Cutting back just a little caused more growth and recovery, which equals more mass and shape. Now I usually do three exercises for the biceps. You have to gauge how much your biceps can take in your training cycle."[3]

Mike Francois on arm training:
"I still consider the basics to be the best way for a beginner to build a solid base for massive biceps. The old analogy that you must first lay a foundation before you build a house holds true for bodybuilding progress. A primary mis-

Stretching:
Stretching is a crucial activity on non-training days. Spend several minutes stretching the biceps and triceps muscles every day. Many bodybuilders consider stretching a crucial ingredient in building better arms.

Measurements:
Check your arm measurements at least once a month. This will give you an idea of whether or not your current arm training routine is providing progress. Additionally, use the mirror often to find out if new size and shape is occurring in your arms. Don't just focus on big gains. Several small gains over a period of time add

take that many novice bodybuilders make is doing too much too early. Again, to get big, you need to train big, but you must do it wisely and progressively."[4]

Steve Reeves basic bodybuilding philosophy:

"Work really hard and condense everything into three workouts a week, but make them very intense workouts. Use deep concentration and lot of effort. In other words, give your total amount of energy to every workout and then rest sufficiently between training sessions to recover and grow. Use as much weight as you can, but only while maintaining strict form...I'd do nine sets per bodypart."[5]

From Dorian Yates, Mr. Olympia:

"Most bodybuilders spend too much time in the gym and don't work out hard enough when they're there."[6]

From Arnold Schwarzenegger:

"I've discovered that arm growth is more rapid on a twice-a-week program...when training for arm size you must gain weight. Although the exact figure may vary from one person to the next, generally speaking it takes about a 10-pound weight gain to add one inch in arm size."[7]

Dorian wins again!

Samir Bannout, 1983 Mr. Olympia

"I think the combination of heavy poundages and lighter weights has given me better development than would have been possible by just using heavy poundages alone...anyone who wants to work hard can develop sensationally peaked biceps."[8]

Porter Cottrell

Samir Bannout

Porter Cottrell

"I recommend a minimum of three days' rest – 72 hours – before returning to the same bodypart. Anything less and you will almost surely notice that, as workouts progress without rest, fatigue increases at least linearly, sometimes geometrically. Take just one more day's rest, and you'll feel a huge increase in strength and flexibility.. .I always tell beginning bodybuilders that the game of bodybuilding is not actually played in the gym. It's played in the arena of proper eating. To me, nutrition is 95 to 99 percent of recuperation. Even if a bodybuilder trained properly without overtraining, took good care of his body and got plenty of sleep, if he didn't eat right, he'd never recuperate. It's essential that you get sufficient amounts of protein and carbohydrates throughout the day in five or six small meals. That's the foundation of recuperation."[9]

Lee Labrada

"Your goal should be to progressively fatigue the muscle more and more with each succeeding set until the muscle reaches a new threshold of fatigue. This serves as a signal for new growth...when training with real heavy weights, i.e., weights that will permit only six to eight reps, consider resting long enough to catch your breath plus 30 seconds...between sets your breathing meets the body's demand for oxygen. This is why it is important to rest long enough between sets for your breathing to normalize. If you begin the next set without catching your breath, eventually you will exceed your cardiovascular capacity – i.e. you will run out of breath before the muscle is tired. This is undesirable and unproductive."[10]

Mike Ashley

Mike recognizes the importance of lifting heavy weight for optimum muscle development. But he also realizes the importance of variety in his workouts, and that a person can't stick strictly with heavy weights week in and week out. The muscles need different types of stress, and recuperation time to adapt to the stress.[11]

Lee Haney, Mr. Olympia eight times

"It's very beneficial to constantly vary my arm programs from one workout to the next. This allows me to keep my muscles off-balance and unable to adapt to a set routine, and it helps my biceps to continue increasing in mass and impressiveness."[12]

Aaron Baker

"My workouts consist of three biceps exercises. In the past I did four, but I developed better with less. If you read the arm routines in *Flex*, you'll see that the bodybuilders with the biggest arms do fewer sets and exercises, but with more intensity."[13]

The Keys

Aaron sums up the keys to build arms well — fewer sets and exercises, with much more intensity. That is how you build animal arms.

1. Reg Bradford, interview with Don Long in *Muscular Development*, March 1996, p. 70
2. Reg Bradford, "Peaked Pillars of Power", *Muscular Development*, March, 1996, p. 73
3. Ibid
4. Mike Francois, "Ungodly Guns", *Flex*, January 1996, p. 54
5. John Little, "Crossover Legend", *Flex*, January 1993, p. 52
6. Bill Geiger & Dorian Yates, "How I won the Mr. Olympia," *Muscle & Fitness*, January 1996, p. 73
7. John Little, "Guns from Olympus", *Flex*, January 1993, p. 27
8. Ibid, p. 30
9. Porter Cottrell, Encyclopedia of Recuperation, *Flex*, January 1993, p. 122
10. Labrada's Corner by Lee Labrada, *Muscular Development*, December 1995, p. 96-97
11. Gayle Hall, "Mike Ashley's Triceps," *MuscleMag International*, December 1990, p. 38
12. John Little, "Guns from Olympus," p. 81
13. Aaron Baker, "Deliberate Contractions," *Flex*, August 1990, p. 64

Aaron Baker

INDEX

PHOTO INDEX